Mary Sexton

11

# THE GLORIES of MARY

**About the Editor:** Msgr. Charles J. Dollen, pastor of St. Gabriel's Church, Poway, California, is a contributing editor and columnist for *The Priest* magazine and the author of several titles including the Catholic Digest Book Club Selection, *My Rosary: Its Power and Mystery* (Alba House, 1988).

# THE GLORIES of MARY

## St. Alphonsus Liguori

Edited and abridged by Msgr. Charles Dollen

ALBA · HOUSE   alba house   NEW · YORK

SOCIETY OF ST. PAUL. 2187 VICTORY BLVD . STATEN ISLAND. NEW YORK 10314

*Library of Congress Cataloging-in-Publication Data*

Liguori, Alfonso Maria de'. Saint, 1696-1787.
        [Glorie di Maria. English. Selections]
        The glories of Mary / by Alphonsus Liguori : abridged and edited
by Charles, Dollen.
              p.      cm.
        Abridged translation of: Le glorie di Maria.
        ISBN 0-8189-0561-1
        1. Mary, Blessed Virgin, Saint — Prayer-books and devotions —
English.  I.  Dollen, Charles.   II.  Title.
BX2160.A2L54   1990                                    90-33219
        232.91 — dc20                                      CIP

Designed, printed and bound in the United States of
America by the Fathers and Brothers of the
Society of St. Paul, 2187 Victory Boulevard,
Staten Island, New York 10314, as part of their
communications apostolate.

**Printing Information:**

Current Printing - first digit   1   2   3   4   5   6   7   8   9   10   11   12

Year of Current Printing - first year shown
   1990      1991      1992      1993      1994      1995      1996      1997

*This abridged edition*
*of*
*The Glories of Mary*
*is dedicated*
*to*
Mrs. Filomena Montello

# Table of Contents

## PART ONE
## EXPLANATION OF THE SALVE REGINA

## PART TWO
## DISCOURSES ON THE PRINCIPAL FEASTS OF MARY

## PART THREE
## THE SORROWS OF MARY

## REFLECTIONS
## ON EACH OF THE SEVEN SORROWS OF MARY

## PART FOUR
### THE VIRTUES OF THE MOST BLESSED VIRGIN MARY

## PART FIVE
### PRACTICES OF DEVOTION
### IN HONOR OF THE BLESSED MOTHER

# Preface

The Life of St. Alphonsus Liguori is summed up quite brilliantly in *The Catholic Encyclopedia* in this way: "Theologian, founder of the Congregation of the Most Holy Redeemer (Redemptorists), bishop, Doctor of the Church; born Marienella, near Naples, September 27, 1696; died at Pagani, near Salerno, August 1, 1787. Feast, August 1."

These statistics only begin to tell the story of a man who graduated from the University of Naples at the age of 16 with a doctorate in both civil and canon law. He practiced law for ten years until he began to look at his priestly vocation. He went into home mission work in the countryside of his native territory, and eventually, after many struggles and difficulties, founded the Redemptorists, dedicated to giving parish missions.

He was appointed bishop of St. Agatha of the Goths and was consecrated in Rome, June 20, 1762. Stricken with a debilitating disease in 1768, he was allowed to retire from his bishopric in 1775. He spent the rest of his life at the house of the Redemptorsits in Pagani.

His writings were voluminous, numbering over 100 books. When the number of editions, revisions, translations of his works, and editions by other writers, are totaled, the number exceeds 4,000.

Considered by some as the "Father of Moral Theology," his major work was his manual of Moral Theology, which he

constantly refined and revised. It has set the tone for the teaching of morality in Cathoic seminaries. It is noteworthy for its
insistence on the value of liberty and free will in man, and the
avoidance of the extremes of the rigorists and the laxists.

Moral theology is the subject for a third of his writings.
Another third are classified as doctrinal works. The remainder
are devotional, and guides for preaching missions in parishes.
The most complete set of the works of St. Alphonsus in English
was published in 1930-31 by the Redemptorist Fathers in
Brooklyn, NY, with Father Eugene Grimm as the editor.

Among the devotional literature provided by St.
Alphonsus, probably his book on visits to the Blessed Sacrament, his Way of the Cross, and *The Glories of Mary* are best
known.

The major portion of *The Glories of Mary* is an explanation
of the famous prayer, the *Salve Regina,* the "Hail Holy Queen."
This is followed by a series of discourses on the major feasts of
the Blessed Mother, and then by reflections on the Seven Dolors,
or Sorrows of Mary. Two very short sections complete the book,
on the virtues of Mary and devotions to Mary.

In the first section, Alphonsus pictures heaven as a vast and
complex imperial court. This would have been very familiar to
him, since he grew up in the Kingdom of Naples and was quite
aware of its working and intrigues. Thus he easily places Mary as
the great and vital power behind the throne. It also explains
much of the seemingly extravant imagery and language that he
uses.

In this, of course, he follows the example of St. John the
Evangelist in his Book of Revelation in the New Testament, who
pictured heaven as a vast and intricate temple with its powerful
liturgy and worship.

These images would have been very familiar and useful to
the readers of his day. If they seem less powerful to us, it explains
why an edition such as this one is offered to you. I have tried to

be true to the spirit and teachings of St. Alphonsus, while moderating the language and imagery. I hope that I do not have to subtitle this introduction, "With apologies to St. Alphonsus"!

St. Alphonsus has been "blamed" for making Mary too important in our devotional life. He would be amazed to think that she could be exaggerated. In the one timeless, eternal decree that occasioned the Incarnation, Mary, with her free consent, is integral. Alphonsus never lost sight of that and he states it clearly and often. With that understood, he lets his love for the Mother of God take off to superb heights.

It should be noted that Alphonsus uses a copy of the Vulgate Bible for his many scriptural quotations. The modern translations which rely heavily on the Greek manuscripts do not always relate the same nuances that Alphonsus used. Therefore, I have used the Douay-Rheims-Challoner translation to be more faithful to the spirit of this work.

# The Salve Regina

Hail Holy Queen, Mother of Mercy, hail our life, our sweetness, and our hope. To you we cry, poor banished children of Eve. To you we send up our sighs, mourning and weeping in this valley of tears. Turn then, most gracious advocate, your eyes of mercy toward us. And after this, our exile, show us Jesus, the blessed fruit of your womb. O clement, O loving, O sweet Virgin Mary!

# To Jesus and Mary

Most loving Redeemer and Lord Jesus Christ, I, your unworthy servant, well knowing what pleasure he gives you who endeavors to exalt your most holy Mother, whom you love so much; knowing too how much you desire to see her loved and honored by all, have determined to publish this work which treats of her glories. I do not know to whom I could better recommend it than to you who so has her glory at heart.

Shower down on all who read it a great love and confidence in this Immaculate Vigin. In her you have placed our hope and refuge, that all the redeemed may share her intercession.

And now, dear Lady, you know that all the gifts I have received from God have come through your powerful intercession. As a mark of my gratitude, I have always encouraged devotion to you, in public and in private. Help me to continue to do so until my dying breath.

Then after my death may this little work continue to preach and teach the greatness of your mercy and love. Help those who use it carry on this great work.

*Your loving though unworthy servant,*
*Alphonsus de Liguori*

# Introduction

*My beloved readers, brothers and sisters in Mary:*

The devotion that prompted me to write this work is the same devotion that prompts you to read it. However, it might be said that there are already enough books about Mary to fulfill all the needs of devout clients of Mary.

I reply in the words of Abbot Francone: "The praise of Mary is an inexhaustible fountain: the more it is enlarged the fuller it gets, and the more you fill it, the more it is enlarged." In short, this Blessed Virgin is so great and so sublime, that the more she is praised, the more there remains to be praised.

Here, I have tried to collect, from as many authors as possible, the choicest passages that promote the love of Mary. I also hope that it will help priests when they preach on this subject.

Worldly lovers often speak of those whom they love, and praise them, so that the object of their affection may be praised and extolled by others. So with those who love Mary, for they take every opportunity to enkindle the flame of love for her, both in public and in private.

St. Bonaventure says that those who make a point of announcing to others the glories of Mary are certain of heaven. "Rejoice then," he exclaims, "rejoice, my soul, and be glad in her;

for how many good things are prepared for those who praise her."

Through his preaching of love for the Mother of God, St. Bernardine of Siena sanctified Italy, and in the same way, St. Dominic converted many provinces. St. Louis Bertrand never omitted in his sermons, exhortations to love Mary, and many others saints have done the same.

In the missions we (Redemptorists) preach, it is an inviolable rule that one sermon be on devotion to Mary. The topic that is most effective is the one on the mercy of Mary. I say on her mercy, for as St. Bernard teaches: "We praise her virginity, we admire her humility; but because we are poor sinners, mercy attracts us more and tastes sweeter; we embrace mercy more lovingly; we remember it oftener, and invoke it more earnestly."

Her merciful and most powerful intercession is admirably portrayed in the prayer "Salve Regina," the recital of which is a frequent option in the priestly Office and a great favorite of the devout.

Therefore, the plan of this work is that I shall divide and explain this great prayer in separate chapters. In addition, I will add some thoughts on the principal festivities and virtues of the Mother of God.

# PART ONE
# EXPLANATION OF THE SALVE REGINA

# CHAPTER I

# SALVE REGINA, MATER MISERICORDIA

*Hail, Holy Queen, Mother of Mercy*

*i*

### HOW GREAT SHOULD OUR CONFIDENCE BE IN MARY, THE QUEEN OF MERCY

As the glorious Virgin Mary has been raised to the dignity of Mother of the King of kings, it is not without reason that the Church honors her, and wishes her to be honored by all with the glorious title of Queen.

"If the Son is a king," says St. Athanasius, "the Mother who gave birth to Him is rightly and truly considered a Queen and Sovereign." "No sooner had Mary," says St. Bernardine of Siena, "consented to be Mother of the Eternal Word, than she merited by this consent to be made Queen of the world and of all creatures."

He concludes: "As many creatures as there are who serve God, so many they are who serve Mary: for as angels and men, and all things that are in heaven and on earth, are subject to the empire of God, so they are also under the dominion of Mary!"

Mary, then, is a Queen, but, for our common consolation, be it known that she is a Queen so sweet, so clement and so ready to help us in our miseries, that the holy Church wills that we would salute her in this prayer under the title of Queen of Mercy.

"The title of Queen," St. Albert the Great notes, "differs from that of Empress, which implies severity and rigor, in signifying compassion and charity towards the poor." "The greatness of kings and queen," says Seneca, "consists in relieving the wretched." Whereas tyrants, when they reign, have their own good in view, kings should have that of their subjects at heart.

At the consecration of a king, he is anointed with oil, the symbol of mercy, to denote how important mercy is in ruling subjects. They also have to mete out justice to those who are guilty of wrongdoing.

Although Mary is indeed a Queen, she is not a Queen of justice, intent on punishing the wicked but a Queen of mercy, intent only on winning pardon and peace for sinners. This is why the Church insists that we call Mary "the Queen of Mercy."

It is as if Christ, the King of Justice and Mercy, has given half the kingdom to Mary, reserving justice to Himself and mercy to her. Christ will come with His strict and avenging justice on the Last Day. It is Mary, anointed with the oil of gladness, who will temper that with mercy by her maternal intercession.

How aptly does St. Albert the Great apply the history of Queen Esther from the Book of Esther as the type of our Queen Mary! In the fourth chapter of that book, we read that King Ahasuerus had issued a decree which condemned all Jews to death. Mordecai, who had raised Esther, begs her to intervene, to save their race.

When she declines, fearing that she might bring royal disfavor upon herself, Mordecai reminds her that God has raised her to the throne as the means of saving her people. "Don't think that you, alone of all the Jews, will escape because you are in the king's house," he tells her.

Eventually she stood before Ahasuerus and pleaded for her people: "If I have found favor with you, O King, give me my people, for whom I ask." Ahasuerus, then, through love for Esther, granted her request and decreed salvation for the Jews.

How, then, can God refuse the prayers of Mary, loving her immensely, as He does, when she pleads for her people, the poor, miserable sinners who recommend themselves to her? The Holy Mother of God knows that she is loved by the Holy Trinity. Is it possible that God could refuse her prayers? Each of her prayers is, as it were, an established law for the Lord, that He should show mercy to all for whom she intercedes.

St. Bernard asks: Why does the Church calls Mary "the Queen of Mercy"? And he replies: "It is because we believe that she opens the abyss of the mercy of God to whomsoever she wills, when she wills, and as she wills; so that there is no sinner, however great, who is lost if Mary intercedes for him."

But perhaps we may fear that Mary would not deign to interpose for some sinners, because they are so overloaded with crimes? Or perhaps we ought to be overawed at the majesty and holiness of this great Queen?

"No," says Pope St. Gregory VII, "for the higher and more holy she is, the greater is her sweetness and compassion towards sinners, who have recourse to her with the desire to amend their lives." And we can add with St. Bernard, "Why should human frailty fear to go to Mary? In her there is no austerity, nothing terrible; she is all sweetness, offering support to all."

Suetonius relates of the Emperor Titus, that he could not refuse a favor, so much so that he often promised more than he could grant. He felt that a prince should never send a person away dissatisfied.

Our Queen cannot deceive, and can obtain all that she wills for her clients. When the repentant sinner approaches her, that person can be sure to be heard by her. "Who," says St. Bonaventure, "are the subjects of mercy, if not the miserable?" Have pity, then, on us, O Queen of Mercy, and help us along the way of salvation.

"Say not, O holy Virgin," exclaimed St. George of Nicomedia, "that you cannot assist us on account of the number of our sins, for your power and your compassion are such, that no number of sins, however great, can outweigh them. Nothing resists your power, for our common Creator, honoring you as His Mother, considering your glory as His own . . . exults in fulfilling your petitions as if He were paying a debt."

This means that, although Mary is under an infinite obligation to the Son for having chosen her to be His Mother, yet it cannot be denied that the Son is under great obligation to her for having given Him his humanity; and therefore Jesus, to pay as it were what He owes to Mary, and glorifying in her glory, honors her in a special manner by listening to and granting all her petitions.

How great, then, should be our confidence in this Queen, knowing her great power with God, and that she is so rich and full of mercy, that there is no one living on the earth who does not partake in her compassion and favor.

Our Blessed Lady herself revealed this to St. Bridget, saying: "I am the Queen of heaven and the Mother of Mercy; I am the joy of the just and the door through which sinners are brought to God. There is no sinner on earth so accursed as to be deprived of my mercy."

## PRAYER

*O Mother of my God, and my Lady Mary, as a beggar presents himself before a great queen, so do I present myself before you, the Queen of heaven and earth. From your lofty throne do not hesitate to look at me. God has made you rich so that you may help the poor, and He has made you the Mother of Mercy so that you can help the miserable.*

*I know that I merit nothing, and that I deserve to be deprived of help because of my past ingratitude for God's graces. In your mercy, take me into your service and help me be one of your most loving and faithful servants. O exalted Virgin, Queen of the Universe, help me in this desire to serve you more faithfully.*

## ii

### HOW MUCH OUR CONFIDENCE IN MARY SHOULD BE INCREASED BECAUSE SHE IS OUR MOTHER

It is not without a meaning, or by chance, that Mary's clients call her Mother; indeed, they seem unable to invoke her under any other name, and never tire of calling her Mother. She is certainly our Mother spiritually.

Sin, by depriving our souls of divine grace, deprived them also of life. Jesus, our Redeemer, with an excess of mercy and love, came to restore this life by His own death on the cross, as He Himself declared: "I have come that they may have life, and may have it more abundantly." (Jn 10:10)

He says "more abundantly," for, according to theologians, the benefit of redemption far exceeds the injury of Adam's sin. By reconciling us with God, He made Himself the Father of souls in the law of grace, as was foretold by the prophet Isaiah: "He shall be called the Father of the world to come, the Prince of Peace." (9:6)

Since Jesus is the Father of our souls, Mary is also their Mother: for she, by giving us Jesus, gave us true life; and afterwards, by offering the life of her Son on Mount Calvary for our salvation, she brought us forth to the life of grace.

According to the Fathers, Mary became our Mother on two occasions.

The first, according to St. Albert the Great, was when she merited to conceive the Son of God in her virginal womb. St. Bernardine of Siena says the same more distinctly by telling us that: When at the Annunciation, the most Blessed Virgin gave the consent which was expected by the Eternal Word before becoming her Son, she from that moment asked our salvation of God with intense ardor, and took it to heart in such a way, that from that moment, as a most loving mother, she bore us in her womb."

St. Luke the Evangelist, speaking of the birth of our Blessed Redeemer, says that Mary "brought forth her first-born son." (2:7) It is according to revealed faith that Mary had no other children according to the flesh, so she had many spiritual children and we are those children.

This was revealed by our Lord to St. Gertrude who was one day reading the above text and was perplexed and could not understand how Mary, being only the Mother of Jesus, could be said to have brought forth her first-born. God explained it to her, saying that Jesus was Mary's first-born according to the flesh, but that all mankind were her second-born according to the spirit.

The second occasion on which Mary became our spiritual Mother, and brought us forth to the life of grace, was when she offered to the eternal Father the life of her beloved Son on Mount Calvary, with so bitter sorrow and suffering. St. Augustine declares that: "As she then and there cooperated by her love in the birth of the faithful to the life of grace, she became the spiritual Mother of all who are members of the one Head, Christ Jesus."

It was on Calvary that this most Blessed Virgin brought us forth, by her sorrows, to eternal life: thus we can all call ourselves the children of the sorrows of Mary. Our most loving Mother was always, and in all ways, united to the will of God.

"Therefore," says St. Bonaventure, "when she saw the love of the Eternal Father towards men to be so great that, in order to save them, He willed the death of His Son; and on the other hand, seeing the love of the Son in wishing to die for us: in order to conform herself to this excess of love of both the Father and the Son towards the human race, she also with her entire will offered and consented to the death of her Son in order that we might be saved."

It is true that, according to Isaiah, Jesus, in dying for the redemption of the human race chose to be alone: "The wine press I have trodden alone." (63:3) Seeing the ardent desire of Mary to aid in the salvation of mankind, He disposed it so that she, by the sacrifice and offering of the life of her Jesus, should cooperate in our salvation, and so become the Mother of our souls.

This our Savior signified, when, before expiring, He looked down from the cross on His Mother and on the disciple St. John, who stood at its foot, and, first addressing Mary, He said, "Behold your Son" (Jn 19:26); as it were saying: Behold the whole human race, which by the offer you make of my life for the salvation of all, is even now being born to the life of grace.

Then, turning to the disciple, He said, "Behold your Mother." (Jn 19:26) "By these words," says St. Bernardine of Siena, "Mary, by reason of the love she bore them, became the Mother, not only of St. John, but of all mankind." As the Gospel tells the story, Jesus did not address John as a particular person, but as "the disciple," signifying that He gave Mary as Mother to all who were His disciples, to all Christians.

O blessed are they who live under the protection of so loving and powerful a Mother! The prophet David, although she was not born yet, sought salvation from God by dedicating himself as a son of Mary and thus prayed, "Save the son of your handmaid." (Ps 86:16) "Of what handmaid?" asks St. Augustine; and he answers: "Of her who said: Behold the handmaid of the Lord." (Lk 1:38)

"And who," says St. Robert Bellarmine, "would ever dare to snatch these children from the bosom of Mary, when they have taken refuge there? What power of hell, or what temptation, can overcome them, if they place their confidence in the patronage of this great Mother, the Mother of God and of themselves?"

Our Blessed Lady herself, in a vision, addressed these words to St. Bridget: "As a mother on seeing her son in the midst of the swords of his enemies, would use every effort to save him, so do I, and I will do for all sinners who seek my mercy."

Thus it is in every engagement with the powers of hell, we shall always certainly conquer by having recourse to the Mother of God, who is also our Mother, saying and repeating again and again, "We fly to your patronage, O holy Mother of God: we fly to your patronage, O holy Mother of God." How many victories the faithful have gained by using this short but powerful prayer!

Be of good heart, then, all you who are children of Mary. Remember, she accepts as her children all who choose to be so. Rejoice! Why do you fear to be lost when such a Mother defends and protects you. As St. Bonaventure reminds us, "Each person who loves this good Mother and relies on her protection will gain confidence in the knowledge that Jesus is our Brother, and Mary our Mother."

St. Anselm echoes the same joy: "O happy confidence! O safe refuge! the Mother of God is my Mother." How firm, then, should be our confidence, since our salvation depends on the judgment of a good Brother and a tender Mother.

It is Mary our Mother who calls us, using the words of Scripture: "He that is a little one, let him turn to me." (Prov 9:4) Children always have their mother's name on their lips, and in every fear, in every danger, they call out "Mother!" This is precisely the source of our confidence in the intercession of Mary, our Mother.

# PRAYER

*O most holy Mother Mary, you are so holy and I am such a sinner. You are so rich in virtue and I am so poor. If I cannot deserve to be your child, at least number me among your servants.*

*But I am confident in your powerful intercession with your Son. Help me turn to Him with deep repentance and a firm purpose of amendment. Cleansed from sin through His re- deeming death, accept me as your child now and at the hour of my death.  Amen.*

## iii
### THE GREATNESS OF THE LOVE WHICH THIS MOTHER BEARS US

Since Mary is our Mother, we may now consider how great her love is for us. Love towards our children is a necessary impulse of nature. St. Thomas Aquinas says that this is the reason why divine law imposes on children the obligation of loving their parents. It gives no express command that parents love their children since nature itself has so strongly implanted that in all creatures.

As St Ambrose remarks: "We know that a mother will expose herself to danger for her children." Even the most savage beasts cannot do otherwise than love their young. If this is true in nature, says Mary, how can I forget to love you, my children? And even if such a thing were possible, that a mother should forget to love her child, it is impossible that I should cease to love a soul that has become my child. "Can a woman forget her infant, so as not to have pity on the son of her womb? And even if she should forget, yet will I not forget you." (Is 44:15)

Mary is our Mother, not according to the flesh but by love: "I am the Mother of fair love." (Ec 24:24) Hence it is the love she bears for us that makes her our Mother.

Let us consider the reason of this love, for then we shall be better able to understand how much she really loves us.

The first reason for the love that Mary bears us is the great love that she has for God. Love towards God and love towards neighbor belong to the same commandment, as expressed by St. John: "This commandment we have from God, that he who loves God, love also his brother." (1 Jn 4:21) As the one becomes greater, the other also increases.

Consider what the saints have done because of their love of God. Read only the account of the labors of St. Francis Xavier in the Indies. See St. Francis de Sales, who, in order to convert unbelievers in the province of Chablais, risked his life every morning for a year. St. Paulinus delivered himself up as a slave, while St. Fidelis of Sigmaringen preached openly about the Church, although he knew it would bring him death.

The saints, then, because they loved God so much, did much for their neighbor. But, who ever loved God as much as Mary? She loved Him more in the first moment of her existence than all the saints and angels ever loved Him, or will love Him.

Among all the blessed spirits, there is not one that loves God more than Mary, so neither do we have nor can we have anyone who, after God, loves us as much as this loving Mother. If we concentrate all the love that mothers bear their children, that husbands and wives have for one another, all the love of angels and saints for their clients, it does not equal the love of Mary towards a single soul.

Moreover, our Mother loves us much because we were recommended to her by her beloved Jesus, when He, before expiring, said to her: "Woman, behold your Son." (Jn 19:26) We were all represented in the person of St. John, as we have already observed. These were among His last words. The last recommendations left before death by persons we love are always treasured and never forgotten.

Again, we are exceedingly dear to Mary on account of the sufferings we cost her. Mothers generally love those children most, the preservation of whose lives has cost them the most suffering and anxiety. We are those children for whom Mary, in order to obtain for us the life of grace, was obliged to endure the bitter agony of herself offering her beloved Jesus to die an ignominious death, and had to see Him expire before her very eyes among the most cruel of torments.

It was, then, by this great offering of Mary that we were born to her to the life of grace. We are, therefore, her very dear children, since we cost her such great suffering. And, thus, as it is written of the love of the Eternal Father towards men, in giving His own Son to death for us, that "God so loved the world as to give His only-begotten Son" (Jn 3:16), "so also," says St. Bonaventure, "we can say of Mary, that she has so loved us as to give her only-begotten Son for us."

Finally, she gave Him for us a thousand and a thousand times during the three hours preceding His death, which she spent at the foot of the cross. During that whole time, she unceasingly offered, with extreme sorrow and the extremes of love, the life of her Son on our behalf.

Because all has been redeemed by Jesus, Mary loves and protects all.

It was she who was seen by St. John in the Book of Revelation: "And a great sign appeared in the heavens: a woman clothed with the sun." (21:1) She is said to be clothed with the sun because as there is no one on earth who can be hidden from the heat of the sun, so there is no one living who can be deprived of the love of Mary.

"And who," exclaims St. Antoninus, "can ever form an idea of the tender care that this most loving mother takes of all of us . . . offering and dispensing her mercy to everyone." Our good mother desired the salvation of all and cooperated in obtaining it.

"It is evident," writes St. Bernard, "that she was solicitous for the whole human race." Thus many of Mary's clients ask God to give them the graces that the Blessed Virgin knows are best for them.

On this point St. Albert the Great applies these words from the Book of Wisdom to Mary: "She hastens to make herself known in anticipation of men's desire; he who watches for her at dawn shall not be disappointed, for he shall find her sitting by his gate." (6:13-14) Mary anticipates those who have recourse to her by making them find her before they seek her. She comes before she is called.

And now, if Mary is so good to all, even to the ungrateful and negligent, who love her but little, and seldom have recourse to her, how much more loving will she be to those who love her and call upon her often. "O how easy," adds the same St. Albert, "it is for those who love Mary to find her, and to find her full of compassion and love!"

In the words of the Book of Proverbs, "I love those who love me." (8:17) As St. Bernard remarks: "She recognizes and loves those who love her more tenderly." Blessed Raymond Jordan adds that: "Those who love Mary are not only loved by her, but served by her." According to St. John Berchmans of the Society of Jesus: "If I love Mary I am certain of perseverance, and shall obtain whatever I wish from God."

O, how much does the love of this good Mother exceed that of all her children. Let them love her as much as they will,

Mary is always among lovers the most loving, says St. Ignatius the Martyr.

St. Stanislaus Kostka loved this dear mother so tenderly that he always spoke of her as if he were addressing her face to face. When the *Salve Regina* was sung, his whole countenance lighted up as if he were inflamed with love.

Indeed, the saints offer us much encouragement in loving Mary. St. Philip Neri called her his delight. St. Bernard called her the ravisher of hearts. Each day St. Bernardine of Siena visited a shrine of Mary, as one would visit a friend or a lover.

St. Aloysius Gonzaga rejoiced to hear the name of Mary. St. Francis of Solano sang at her shrines as if serenading a lover. Charles, the son of St. Bridget, said that nothing consoled him as much as the knowledge that Mary was so greatly loved by God.

St. Alphonsus Rodriguez offered to lay down his life as a testimony of his love for Mary. St. Peter Damian claimed that Mary loved us "with an invincible love." St. Bonaventure claimed that it was a mark of good fortune to have a special love for Mary.

Let us cry out with St. Anselm: "May my heart languish and my soul melt and be consumed with your love, O my beloved Savior Jesus, and my dear Mother Mary!"

## PRAYER

*Mother Mary, you have enamored God with the spiritual beauty He caused in your soul. Now draw us into the circle of your love and let us be devoted sons and daughters of so special a Mother.*

*Let me love you with all the powers of my soul, my mind and my body. Through this love lead me ever more truly into the love of Jesus, your Son.*

*Show your great mercy to me, a sinner, and lead me to true repentance in the ways that please your Son, Jesus Christ.*


## iv

### MARY IS THE MOTHER OF PENITENT SINNERS

Our Blessed Lady told St. Bridget that she was the Mother not only of the just and the innocent, but also of sinners, provided they were willing to repent. How promptly does a sinner, desirous of amendment and recommending himself to her, find that this Mother embraces him and helps him, far more than any earthly mother!

Pope Gregory VII wrote in this sense to the princess Matilda, saying: "Resolve to sin no more and I promise that you will undoubtedly find Mary more ready to love you than any earthly mother."

But whoever aspires to be a child of this great Mother must first abandon sin and then may hope to be accepted as such. St. Peter Chrysologus says that he who acts in a different manner from Mary, declares thereby that he will not be her son. "He who does not the works of his mother, abjures his lineage."

Mary humble, and he proud; Mary pure, and he wicked; Mary full of love, and he hating his neighbor. Thus he proves that he is not, and will not, be the son of his holy Mother. The children of Mary must be imitators of her. A certain sinner once prayed, "Show yourself a Mother"; but the Blessed Virgin replied, "Show yourself a son." Indeed, "He is cursed of God who angers his mother." (Ec3:18)

That is spoken of the obstinate sinner. If a sinner, though he hasn't given up his sins, seeks the help of Mary to help him avoid sin, this good Mother will not fail to assist him in recovering the grace of God. This is precisely what St. Bridget heard from the lips of Jesus Christ, who, speaking to his mother said:

"You always assist him who tries to return to God, and your help is never wanting to him."

So long, then, as a sinner is obstinate, Mary cannot love him; but if he, finding himself chained by some passion which keeps him a slave of hell, recommends himself to the Blessed Virgin, and implores her, with confidence and perseverance, to help him withdraw from the state of sin in which he is, there can be no doubt that this good Mother will extend her powerful hand to him, will deliver him from his chains, and lead him to a state of salvation.

The teaching that all prayers and works performed in a state of sin are themselves sins, was condemned by the Council of Trent. St. Bernard says that although prayer in the mouth of a sinner lacks beauty, as it is unaccompanied by charity, nevertheless it is useful, and obtains grace to abandon sin. It is the opinion of St. Thomas Aquinas that the prayer of a sinner, though without merit, is an act which obtains the grace of forgiveness.

The power of prayer is founded not on the merits of him who asks, but on the divine goodness, and the merits and promises of Jesus Christ who has said: "Every one who asks, receives." (Lk 11:10) St. Anselm applies this to the Blessed Mother: "If he who prays does not merit to be heard, the merits of the Mother, to whom he recommends himself, will intercede effectually."

St. Bernard exhorts all sinners to have recourse to Mary, invoking her with great confidence; for although the sinner does not himself merit the graces which he asks, yet he receives them, because this Blessed Virgin asks and obtains them from God, on account of her own merits.

He writes: "Because you were unworthy to receive the grace yourself, it was given to Mary in order that through her, you might receive all." And he continues:

"If a mother knew that her two sons were mortal enemies to each other, would she not exert herself to her utmost to reconcile them? This would be the duty of a good mother, and it is thus that Mary acts, for she is the mother of Jesus and the Mother of men.

"When she sees a sinner at enmity with Jesus Christ, she cannot endure it and does all in her power to make peace between them. O happy Mary, you are the Mother of the criminal and the Mother of the Judge. Being the Mother of both, they are her children, and you cannot endure discord among them."

This most gracious Lady only requires that the sinner should have a firm purpose of amendment and recommend himself to her. This is exactly what the Blessed Virgin said to St. Bridget: "However much a person sins, I am ready to receive that person immediately, as long as there is repentance. I do not pay any attention to the number of sins, but only to the intention to repent. I do not hesitate to anoint and heal the wounds of sin; for I am called, and truly am, the Mother of Mercy."

Mary is the mother of sinners who wish to repent, and as a mother she cannot do otherwise than be compassionate for them. Rather, she seems to feel the miseries of her poor children as if they were her own.

Take the example of the Canaanite woman. When she begged Our Lord to deliver her daughter from the evil that plagued her, she said, "Have mercy on me, O Lord, Son of David, my daughter is grievously troubled by a devil." (Mt 15:22)

Since the daughter, not the mother, was tormented, she should have begged Him, "Lord, have mercy on my daughter," and not "Have mercy on me." But no, she said, "Have mercy on me," and she was right; the sufferings of children are felt by their mother as if they were their own.

It is precisely thus that Mary prays to God when she recommends a sinner; she cries out for the sinful soul, "Have mercy on me!" "My Lord," she seems to say, "this poor soul that is in sin is my child, therefore pity not so much the sinner as me, the Mother."

Would that all sinners had recourse to this kind Mother, for then certainly all would be pradoned by God. "O Mary," St. Bonaventure exclaims in astonishment, "you embrace with maternal affection a sinner despised by the whole world, and you do not leave him until you have reconciled the poor creature with his Judge!"

Most certainly God will not condemn those sinners who have recourse to Mary, and for whom she prays, since He Himself commended them to her as her children.

As the devout Blosius puts it: "Who can ever tell the goodness, the mercy, the compassion, the love, the benignity, the clemency, the fidelity, the charity, of this Virgin Mother towards men? It is such that no words can express it."

"Let us then," says St. Bernard, "cast ourselves at the feet of this good mother, and embracing them, let us not depart until she blesses us, and so accepts us as her children." Who can ever doubt the compassion of this Mother?

# PRAYER

*O my sovereign Queen and worthy Mother of the Redeemer, most holy Mary; I see myself despicable because of my sins and so hardly dare to call you Mother, or even approach you; yet I will not allow my miseries to deprive me of the consolation and confidence I feel in calling you Mother.*

*I know that you should reject me, but I beg you to remember all that your Son Jesus had endured for me. Then reject me, if you can!*

*I have sinned against the majesty of God, but that is now past. I turn to you with a firm purpose of amendment in my heart, and beg you to intercede for me.*

*Neither on earth nor in heaven can I find one who has more compassion for me, the sinner, or who is better able to assist me, than you, O Mother Mary. O Jesus and Mary, you both love the most miserable, and go seeking them in order to save them.*

*I present myself before you with a certain hope that I shall not be abandoned. Behold me at your feet: my Jesus, forgive me; My Mother Mary, help me!*

# VITA, DULCEDO
## Our Life, Our Sweetness

### i

MARY IS OUR LIFE, BECAUSE SHE OBTAINS FOR US THE
PARDON OF OUR SINS

To understand why holy Church makes us call Mary our life, we
must know that as the soul gives life to the body, so divine grace
gives life to the soul; for a soul without grace has the name of
being alive but is in truth dead, as it was said of one in the Book
of Revelation, "You have the name of being alive, but you are
dead." (3:1) Mary, in helping sinners obtain grace by her intercession, restores them to life.

The Church frequently applies the words of Scripture to
Mary, in a devotional sense. Thus, "Those who watch for me in
the early morning shall find me." (Prov 8:17) Those who seek
Mary in the morning, that is, as soon as they can, will certainly
find her. And a little further on in the same place, "He who finds
me shall find life, and shall have salvation from the Lord." (8:35)

"Listen," exclaims St. Bonaventure, "listen, all you who
desire the kingdom of God: honor the most Blessed Virgin Mary
and you will find life and eternal salvation."

St. Bernardine of Siena is of the opinion that if God did not destroy mankind after the first sin, it was on account of his singular love for this holy Virgin, who was destined to be born of this race. And he adds that he has no doubt "but that all the mercies granted by God under the old dispensation were granted only in consideration of this most Blessed Lady."

Hence St. Bernard was right in exhorting us "to seek for grace, and to seek it by Mary"; meaning that if we had the misfortune to lose the grace of God, we should seek to recover it, but should do so through Mary; for though we may have lost it, she has found it; therefore the saint calls her "the finder of grace."

The Archangel Gabriel expressly declared this for our consolation, when he saluted the Blessed Virgin, saying, "Fear not, Mary, for you have found grace." (Lk 1:30) Since Mary always had grace — "Hail, full of grace, the Lord is with you." (Lk 1:28) — she found grace not for herself but for sinners who have lost it.

Again, we can apply the eighth chapter of the Canticle of Canticles of Mary: "I am a wall and my breasts are as a tower, and therefore I have become in his presence as one finding peace." (8:10) She is truly the mediatrix of peace between sinners and God.

St. Bernard, commenting on these words, encourages sinners, saying: "Go to this Mother of Mercy and show her the wounds which your sins have left on your soul; then she will certainly entreat her Son, by the breasts that nourished Him, to pardon you for everything. This divine Son who loves her so tenderly, will most certainly grant her petition."

It is in this sense that the holy Church, in almost daily prayers, calls upon us to beg our Lord to grant us the powerful help of the intercession of Mary to help us rise from our iniquities.

With reason, then, St. Lawrence Justinian calls her "the hope of malefactors," since she alone is the one who obtains pardon for them from God. Others have called her "the sinners' ladder," and "the only hope of sinners."

St. John Chrysostom addresses this prayer to her: "Hail, Mother of God and of us all, 'heaven' where God dwells, 'throne' from which our Lord dispenses all graces: 'fair daughter, Virgin, honor, glory and firmament of our Church,' assiduously pray to Jesus that in the day of judgment we may find mercy through you, and receive the reward prepared by God for those who love Him."

With reason, finally, Mary is called, in the words of the Canticle, the dawn: "Who is she that comes forth as the rising dawn?" (6:9) Pope Innocent III says: "For as the dawn is the end of the night and the beginning of the day, well may the Blessed Virgin Mary, who was the end of vices, be called the dawn of day."

When devotion to Mary begins in a soul, it produces the same effect that the birth of this most Holy Virgin produced in the world. It puts an end to the night of sin and leads the soul into the bright light of the path to virtue. Therefore St. Germanus prayed: "O Mother of God, your protection never ceases, your intercession is life and your patronage never fails."

We read in the Gospel of St. Luke, that Mary said: "Behold, from this time on, all generations will call me blessed." (1:48) "Yes, my Lady," exclaims St. Bernard, "all generations shall call you blessed for you have begotten life and glory for all generations of mankind. In you sinners find pardon, and the just perseverance and eternal life." For this cause all shall call you blessed, for all your servants obtain, through you, the life of grace and eternal glory.

St. Andrew of Crete calls Mary the pledge of divine mercy, meaning that, when sinners have recourse to Mary, they may be reconciled with God and be assured of pardon and peace. Mary is this pledge which God had bestowed on us for our advocate, and by whose intercession, by virtue of the merits of Jesus Christ, God forgives all who have recourse to her.

St. Bridget heard an angel say that the holy Prophets "exulted, knowing that our Lord Himself would be appeased by the humility and the purity of Mary's life, and that He would be reconciled with those who had provoked His wrath."

Mary is that happy Ark, says St. Bernard, "in which those who take refuge will never suffer the shipwreck of eternal perdition." At the time of the deluge, even brutes were saved in Noah's ark. Under the mantle of Mary, even sinners obtain salvation.

St. Gertrude once saw Mary with her mantle extended, and under it, many wild beasts — lions, bears and tigers — had taken refuge. She remarked that Mary not only did not reject them, but even welcomed them and caressed them with gentle tenderness.

The saint understood by this that the most abandoned sinners who have recourse to Mary are not only not rejected, but that they are welcomed and saved by her from eternal death. Let us, then, enter this Ark, let us take refuge under the mantle of Mary, and she most certainly will help us secure salvation.

## PRAYER

*O Holy Mother of God, behold at your feet a miserable sinner. The whole Church proclaims you the Mother of Mercy and the Refuge of Sinners.*

*You know how much your divine Son desires the salvation of sinners. You know what He endured for this reason. You know His sufferings: the cold chill in the stable, the flight into*

*Egypt, his toil, sweat and blood. You yourself witnessed the anguish He suffered for us on the cross.*

*Show your love for Jesus by extending the hand of your mercy to us for whom He suffered so much. I implore you to assist us to be restored to His presence and His love.*

*Jesus wills that we have recourse to you, not only that His Blood has saved us, but that your prayers may also aid us. Pray for us; tell your Son that you, too, desire our salvation, and God will certainly answer your prayers.*

*Say that I am yours, and then I have obtained all that I ask, all that I desire.*


## ii

### MARY IS ALSO OUR LIFE, BECAUSE SHE OBTAINS FOR US PERSEVERANCE

Final perseverance is so great a gift of God, that, as the Council of Trent teaches, it is quite gratuitous on His part, and we cannot merit it. St. Augustine, however, tells us that all who seek the gift will be given it, if they pursue it diligently until the end of their lives.

St. Robert Bellarmine puts it well then he says: "That which is daily required must be asked for every day." Now, if it is true, as I shall show later in this work, that all the graces that God dispenses to us pass through the hands of Mary, then we can hope for the greatest of all graces — perseverance, through her intercession.

We shall obtain it if we seek it with confidence from Mary. This grace she promises to all who serve her faithfully during life, in the words of Ecclesiasticus, which the Church applies to her on the Feast of the Immaculate Conception: "Those who work by me shall not sin. Those who explain me shall have life everlasting." (24:30)

In order that we may be preserved in the life of grace, we require spiritual fortitude to resist the many enemies of salvation. We are assured that we can obtain this gift through Mary by the words of the Book of Proverbs, which the Church applies to Mary in the Little Office: "Strength is mine; by me kings reign." (8:14)

"Strength is mine" means that God has bestowed this precious gift on Mary so that she may dispense it to her faithful clients. "By me kings reign" signifies that by her means her servants reign over and command their senses and passions, and so become worthy to reign eternally in heaven.

What strength the servants of this Lady possess, to overcome the assualts of hell! She is that tower described in the Canticle: "Your neck is as the tower of David, which is built with bulwarks; a thousand bucklers hang on it, all the armor of valiant men." (4:4)

She is as a well-defended fortress in defense of her lovers, who in their warfare have recourse to her. In her, her clients find all the shields and arms needed to defend themselves against the power of hell.

Mary is also likened to the plane tree in Ecclesiasticus: "As a plane tree by the water was I exalted in the city streets." (24:14) We are told that a plane tree has leaves like shields, an image of Mary who defends all who take refuge in her.

Blessed Amadeus gives another explanation and says that this holy Virgin is called a plane tree, because, as the plane shelters travellers under its branches from the heat of the sun and from the rain, so do men and women find refuge under the mantle of Mary from the ardor of their passions and from the fury of temptations.

Truly are those souls to be pitied who abandon this defense, in ceasing their devotion to Mary, and no longer recommending themselves to her in times of danger. If the sun ceased to rise, says St. Bernard, how could the world become other than a chaos of darkness and horror?

Applying his question to Mary, he repeats it: "Take away the sun and where will be the day? Take away Mary, and what will be left but the darkest night?"

When a soul loses devotion to Mary, it is immediately enveloped in darkness, and it is in that darkness of which the Holy Spirit speaks in the Psalms: "You bring darkness and it is night; then all the beasts of the forest roam about." (104:20)

When the light of heaven ceases to shine in a soul, all is darkness, and it becomes the haunt of devils and of every sin. St. Anselm says that "If any one is disregarded and condemned by Mary, he is necessarily lost." Therefore we may exclaim with reason, "Woe to those who despise its light!" that is to say, all who despise devotion to Mary.

St. Francis Borgia always doubted the perseverance of those in whom he did not find particular devotion to the Blessed Virgin. When he questioned novices about their devotion to the saints, if he found some who did not have devotion to Mary, he charged the novice-master to keep special watch over them. He doubted the sincerity of their religious vocations.

St. Germanus called the Blessed Virgin the "breath of Christians." As he put it: "As breathing is not only a sign but even a cause of life, so the name of Mary, which is constantly found on the lips of God's servants, both proves that they are truly alive, and at the same time causes and preserves their life, and gives them every help."

Blessed Alan was once assaulted by a violent temptation and was on the point of yielding, for he had not recommended himself to Mary, when the most Blessed Virgin appeared to him, and in order that he might remember to invoke her aid, she gave him a blow, saying, "If you had recommended yourself to me, you would not have run into such danger."

The Church frequently applies these words from the Book of Proverbs to Mary: "Happy the man watching daily at my gates, waiting at my doorposts." (8:34) It is as if she would say, "Blessed is he that hears my voice and is constantly attentive to apply at the door of my mercy, and seeks light and help from me." For clients who do this, Mary does her part, and obtains for them the light and strength they need to abandon sin and advance in virtue.

Pope Innocent III calls her "the moon at night, the dawn at break of day, and the sun at mid-day." She is a moon to enlighten those who blindly wander in the night of sin and makes them see and understand the miserable state of damnation in which they are. She is the dawn, the forerunner of the sun, to those whom she has already enlightened, and makes them abandon sin and return to God, the true sun of justice. Finally, she is a sun to those who are in a state of grace, and prevents them from falling again over the precipice of sin.

Learned writers apply these word from Ecclesiasticus to her, "Her bonds are a saving binding." (6:30) "Why bonds?" asks St. Lawrence Justinian: "Because she binds her clients to herself to prevent them from straying into the paths of vice."

She not only helps them avoid sin, but she leads them to virtue, the virtues both of her Son and of her own. Persevering in these virtues is her particular concern for her clients.

Therefore, St. Philip Neri used to exhort his penitents: "My children, if you desire perseverance, be devout to our Blessed Lady." St. John Berchmans of the Society of Jesus also used to repeat: "Whoever loves Mary will have perseverance."

O, if only all people loved this most kind and loving Lady! If they always had recourse to her, and without delay in their temptations, who would fall? He falls and is lost who does not have recourse to Mary.

St. Thomas of Villanova gives a touching and child-like example. When we are tempted by the devil, we should imitate little chicks. As soon as they perceive the approach of a hawk, they run under the wings of their mother hen for protection. Thus, we should not stop to reason with temptation, but fly immediately under the mantle of Mary.

St. Bernard reminds us: "Whoever you are, in this world you are tossed about on a stormy and tempestuous sea. You do not walk on solid ground. In the midst of the storm, look to the brightest star, call upon Mary. In dangers, in difficulties, in doubts, remember Mary, call upon Mary."

He adds: "Following her, you will certainly not go astray. Imploring her, you will not sink into despair. If she supports you, you cannot fail."

# PRAYER

*In you, O Mother of God, I have unbounded confidence. From you I hope for the grace to bewail my sins as I ought, and from you I hope for the strength never to fall into them again.*

*If I am sick, be a heavenly physician for me and heal me. Since my sins have weakened me, your help will strengthen me. O Mary, I hope all from you, for you are all powerful with God. Amen.*

## iii
### MARY OUR SWEETNESS; SHE RENDERS DEATH SWEET TO HER CLIENTS

"He who is a friend is always a friend and a brother is proved in time of distress." (Prov 17:17) We can never know our friends and relatives in the time of prosperity; it is only in the time of adversity that we see them in their true colors.

People of the world never abandon a friend as long as he is prosperous. Should misfortunes overtake him, and more particularly at the point of death, they immediately forsake him.

Mary does not act thus with her clients. In their afflictions, and particularly in the sorrows of death, the greatest that can be endured in this world, this good Lady and Mother not only does not abandon her faithful servants, but as, during our exile, she is our life, so also is she, at our last hour, our sweetness, by obtaining for us a calm and happy death.

From that day on which Mary had the privilege and the sorrow of being present at the death of Jesus her Son, who is the head of all the predestined, it became her privilege to assist also at our deaths.

For this reason, holy Church teaches us to beg this most Blessed Virgin to assist us, especially at the moment of death. We conclude the Hail Mary, one of our most familiar and most used prayers: Pray for us sinners, now and at the hour of our death!

O how great are the sufferings of the dying! They suffer from remorse of conscience on account of past sins, from fear of the approaching judgment, and from the uncertainty of their eternal salvation.

Then it is that hell arms itself, and spares no efforts to gain the soul which is on the point of entering eternity; for it knows that only a short time remains in which to gain it.

"But woe to you, earth and sea, for the Devil has come down to you in great fury, for he knows he has but a short time." (Rev 12:12) For this reason, the enemy of our salvation, whose charge it was to tempt the soul during life, does not choose at death to be alone, but calls others to his assistance, according to the prophet Isaiah: "Their house shall be filled with serpents." (13:21)

And indeed, such they are. For when a person is at the

point of death, the whole place in which he is, is filled with devils, who all unite to make him lose his soul.

But how quickly do the rebellious spirits flee from the presence of Mary, the Queen of Heaven. If at the hour of death we have the protection of Mary, what need we fear from all our infernal enemies?

When King David trembled at the thought of death, he prayed, "Even though I walk in the dark valley I fear no evil; for you are at my side with your rod and your staff to give me courage." (Ps 23:4) The staff signifies the cross of Christ and the all-sufficient merits which Christ won for us on it, while the rod signifies the intercession of Mary.

"The mother of God," says St. Peter Damian "is that powerful rod with which the violence of the infernal enemies is conquered." Indeed, how many of the saints and those of blessed memory were granted visions of this Blessed Mother at the hour of their death.

St. Bonaventure pictures Mary sending St. Michael with all the angels to defend her dying servants. Addressing our Lady, he says: "Michael, the leader and prince of the heavenly hosts, with all the administering spirits, obeys your command, and defends and receives the souls of the faithful who have particularly recommended themselves to you, O Lady."

St. Jerome, writing to the virgin Eustochia, says: "What a day of joy that will be for you, when Mary, the Mother of our Lord, accompanied by the choirs of virgins, will go to meet you." The Blessed Virgin assured St. Bridget of this; for speaking of her devout clients at the point of death, she said: "Then will I, their dear Lady and Mother, fly to them, that they may have consolation and refreshment."

St. Vincent Ferrer says that not only does the most Blessed Virgin console and refresh them, but that "she receives the souls of the dying." This loving Queen takes them under her mantle, and thus presents them to the Judge, her Son, and most certainly obtains their salvation.

We are told by St. Bridget that this is exactly what happened to her son, Charles, who died while in the army. She feared much for her son, who was exposed to all the temptations and dangers of a young man in the military.

But the Blessed Virgin revealed to her that he was saved on account of his love for her, and that she herself had assisted him at the hour of his death, and had suggested to him what acts to make at that most important moment in his life.

At the same time, St. Bridget saw Jesus on His throne, and the devil bringing two accusations against the Blessed Virgin. The first was that Mary had prevented him from tempting Charles at the moment of death, and the second was that Mary had herself presented his soul to the Judge. Bridget then saw the Judge drive the devil away and bring Charles into heaven.

You, devout reader, will, without doubt, experience the same joy and contentment in death, if you can then remember that you have loved this good Mother, who cannot be otherwise than faithful to her children who have been faithful in serving and honoring her, by their visits, rosaries, fasts, almsgiving and especially in recommending themselves to her intercession with Christ every day.

Nor will this consolation be withheld from you, even if for a time you have been a sinner, provided that, from this day, you are careful to live well a Christian life and to serve this most gracious Lady, his Mother, our Queen.

Let us then be of good heart, though we be sinners, and feel certain that Mary will assist us at the hour of our death. Mary addressed St. Matilda on this point: "I, as a most tender Mother, will faithfully be present at the death of all who piously serve me, and will console and protect them."

O God, what a consolation it will be at that last moment in our lives, when our eternal lot is so soon to be decided, to see the

Queen of Heaven assisting and consoling us with the assurance of her protection.

## PRAYER

*O my most sweet Mother, how shall I die, poor sinner that I am? Even now, the thought of that important moment when I must expire, and appear before the judgment seat of God, and the remembrance that I have so often written out my own condemnation, makes me tremble.*

*In the Blood of Jesus, and in your maternal intercession, I find reason to hope.*

*You are the Queen of Heaven, the mistress of the universe, in short, you are the Mother of God. Your noble and loving heart embraces us. You bring us, hand in hand, to Jesus the Judge. What can He refuse you, when you plead for us?*

*I thank the Lord for allowing me to know you and serve you with devotion. Now I confidently expect that He will send you from your throne in Heaven to help me at the hour of my death.  Amen.*

CHAPTER III

---

# SPES NOSTRA! SALVE
## *Mary, Our Hope*

---

*i*

MARY IS THE HOPE OF ALL

Modern heretics cannot endure that we should salute and call
Mary our hope: "Hail, our Hope!" they say that God alone is our
hope; and that he curses those who put their trust in creatures in
these words of the prophet Jeremiah: "Cursed be the man that
trusts in man." (17:5)

Mary, they exclaim, is a creature; and how can a creature be
our hope? This is what the heretics say. In spite of this, holy
Church encourages priests and religious to raise their voices, and
in the name of all the faithful invoke and call Mary by the sweet
name of "our Hope," — the hope of all.

The angelical Doctor, St. Thomas Aquinas, says that we
can place our hope in a person in two ways: as a principal cause,
and as a mediate one. Those who hope for a favor from a king,
hope it from him as lord; they hope for it from his minister or a
favorite from him as an intercessor. If the favor is granted it

comes primarily from the king, but it comes through the instrumentality of the favorite; in this case, he who seeks the favor is right in calling his intercessor his hope.

The King of Heaven, being infinite goodness, desires in the highest degree to enrich us with His graces; but because confidence is a requisite on our part, and in order to increase it in us, He had given us His own Mother to be our mother and advocate, and to her He has given all power to help us. Therefore He wills that we should repose our hope of salvation and of every blessing in her.

Those who place their hopes in creatures alone, independently of God, as sinners do, and in order to obtain the friendship and favor of a man fear not to outrage His divine Majesty, are certainly cursed by God, as the prophet Jeremiah says.

But those who hope in Mary, as Mother of God, who is able to obtain graces and eternal life for them, are truly blessed and acceptable to the heart of God, who desires to see the greatest of His creatures honored; for she loved and honored Him in this world more than all men and angels put together.

Therefore, we justly and reasonably call the Blessed Vigin our hope; as St. Robert Bellarmine says: "That we shall obtain, through her intercession, that which we should not obtain by our own unaided prayers."

"We pray to her," says the learned Suarez, "in order that the dignity of the intercessor may supply for our own unworthiness; so that, to implore the Blessed Virgin in such a spirit, is not a lack of trust in the mercy of God, but fear of our own unworthiness."

It is not without reason that holy Church calls Mary "the Mother of holy Hope." She is the Mother who gives birth to holy hope in our hearts; not to the hope of the vain and transitory goods of this life, but of the immense and eternal goods of heaven.

"Hail, then, O hope of my soul!" exclaims St. Ephrem, the Deacon, "hail O certain salvation of Christians; hail O helper of sinners; hail, fortress of the faithful and salvation of the world!"

And reflecting on the present order of Providence, he continues: "O Lady, cease not to watch over us; preserve and guard us under the wings of your compassion and mercy, for, after God, we have no hope but in you." St. Thomas of Villanova repeats the same thing, calling her "our only refuge, help and asylum."

St. Bernard seems to give the reason for this when he says: "See, O man, the designs of God — the designs by which He is able to dispense His mercy more abundantly to us, for desiring to redeem the whole human race. He has placed the whole price of redemption in the hands of Mary, that she may dispense it at will."

Therefore, before the divine Word took flesh in the womb of Mary, He sent an archangel to ask her consent: because He willed that the world should receive the Incarnate Word through her, and that she should be His source of every good.

St. Irenaeus remarks that as Eve was seduced by a fallen angel, to flee from God, so Mary was led to receive God into her womb, obeying a good angel. Thus by her obedience she repaired Eve's disobedience, and became her advocate, and that of the whole human race. "If Eve disobeyed God, yet Mary was persuaded to obey God, that the Virgin Mary might become the advocate of the virgin Eve. And as the human race was bound to death through a virgin, it is saved through a Virgin."

St. Germanus, recognizing in Mary the source of all our good, and that she delivers us from every evil, thus invokes her: "O my sovereign Lady, you are alone the one whom God appointed to be my solace here below; you are the guide of my pilgrimage, the strength of my weakness, the riches of my poverty, remedy for healing my wounds, the soother of my pains, the end of my captivity, the hope of my salvation. Hear my prayers, have pity on my tears, you, my Queen, my refuge, my love, my help, my hope and my strength."

We should not be surprised, then, that St. Antoninus applies the following words from the Book of Wisdom to Mary: "Now all good things come to me together with her." (7:11) For as this Blessed Virgin is the Mother and dispenser of all good things, the whole world, and more particularly each individual who lives in it as a devout client of this great Queen, may say with truth, that with devotion to Mary, both he and the world have obtained everything good and perfect.

O, how many who were once proud have become humble by devotion to Mary; how many who were once irascible have become meek; how many in the midst of darkness have found light; how many who were in despair have found confidence; how many who were lost have found salvation by the same powerful means! And Mary foretold this in the house of Zechariah and Elizabeth: "Behold, from this day forward, all generations shall call me blessed." (Lk 1:48)

St. Bernard, interpreting her words adds: "All generations shall call you blessed because you have given life and glory to all nations, for in you sinners find pardon and the just perseverance in the grace of God."

May the immense goodness of our God be ever praised and blessed for having given us so great, so tender, so loving a Mother and Advocate!

How tender are the sentiments of confidence expressed by St. Bonaventure towards Jesus our most loving Redeemer and Mary our most loving advocate. He says:

"Whatever God foresees to be my lot, I know that He cannot refuse Himself to anyone who loves Him and seeks Him with his whole heart. I will embrace Him with my love; and if He does not bless me, I will still cling to Him so closely that He will be unable to go without me.

"If I can do nothing else, at least I will hide myself in His wounds, and taking up my dwelling place there, it will be in Himself alone that He will find me.

"If my Redeemer rejects me on account of my sins, and drives me from His sacred feet, I will cast myself at those of his beloved Mother, and there I will remain prostrate until she has obtained forgiveness for me; for this Mother of Mercy knows not, and has never known, how to do otherwise than compassionate the miserable and help the most destitute who fly to her for help."

Look down on us then, O most compassionate Mother; cast your eyes of mercy on us, for we are your servants and in you we have placed all our confidence.

## PRAYER

*O Mother of holy love, our life, our refuge and our hope, you well know that your Son Jesus Christ, not content with being Himself our perpetual advocate with the eternal Father, has willed that you should interest yourself with Him, in order to obtain the divine mercies for us.*

*He has decreed that your prayers should aid our salvation, and has made them so efficacious that they obtain all they ask. I trust, then, O Lady, that in the first place through the merits of Jesus Christ, and then through your intercession, that I shall be saved.*

*O Mother of the omnipotent God, tell Him that I am your servant and that you will defend me. Let my dying words be: "Jesus is my only hope, and after Jesus, his Most Blessed Mother, Mary."* Amen.

*ii*

MARY IS THE HOPE OF SINNERS

In the first chapter of the Book of Genesis, we read that "God created two great lights: a greater light to rule the day, and a lesser light to rule the night." (1:16) Some spiritual writers have suggested that the sun symbolizes Christ, the Light of the World who rules over the just. The moon, the lesser light, symbolizes Mary, who enlightens those living in the darkness of sin.

By this symbolism, Mary is the auspicious luminary for the benefit of poor sinners, should anyone be so unfortunate as to fall into the night of sin. Pope Innocent III suggests: "Whoever is in the night of sin, let him cast his eyes on the moon and let him implore Mary."

Since he has lost the light of the sun of justice by losing the grace of God, let him turn to the moon and beseech Mary; she will certainly give him light to see the misery of his state, and strength to leave it without delay. St. Methodius says "that by the prayers of Mary almost innumerable sinners are converted."

One of the titles which is most encouraging to poor sinners, and under which the Church teaches us to invoke Mary in the Litany of Loretto, is that of "Refuge of Sinners." In Judea in ancient times there were cities of refuge, in which criminals who fled there for protection were exempt from the punishments they deserved.

Nowadays these cities are not so numerous; in fact there is but one, and that is Mary, of whom the Psalmist says: "Glorious things are said of you, O city of God." (87:3) This city differs from the ancient ones in this respect — that in the latter all kinds of criminals did not find refuge, nor was the protection extended to every class of crime. Under the mantle of Mary all sinners, without exception, find refuge for every kind of sin that they may have committed, provided only that they go there to seek for this protection.

It is sufficient to have recourse to her, for whoever has the good fortune to enter this city need not speak to be saved. "This city," says St. Albert the Great, "is the most holy Virgin, fenced in with grace and glory." If our sins are so great that we fear Our Lord, let the Blessed Mother intercede for us and ask for what we need.

St. Ephrem salutes Mary thus: "Hail, refuge and hospital of sinners!" St. Basil of Seleucia goes on further: "That if God granted to some who were only His servants such power, that not only their touch but even their shadows healed the sick, who were placed in the public streets for this purpose, how much greater power must we suppose that He has granted to her who was not only His handmaid but His Mother?"

We may indeed say that Our Lord had given us Mary as a public infirmary, in which all who are sick, poor and destitute can be received. But now I ask, in hospitals erected expressly for the poor, who have the greatest claim to admissions? Certainly the most infirm and those who are in the greatest need.

For this reason should anyone find himself devoid of merit and overwhelmed with spiritual infirmities, that is to say, sin, he can address Mary in this way: "O Lady, you are the refuge of the sick poor; reject me not, for as I am the poorest and most infirm of all, I have the greatest right to be welcomed by you."

Let us then cry out with St. Thomas of Villanova: "O Mary, we poor sinners know no other refuge than you, for you are our only hope as an advocate before Jesus. We rely on you for our safety."

In the revelations to St. Bridget, Mary is called the "Star preceding the sun," giving us to understand that when devotion to the blessed Mother begins to manifest itself in a soul that is in a state of sin, it is a certain mark that before long God will enrich it with His grace.

The glorious St. Bonaventure, in order to revive the confidence of sinners in the protection of Mary, places before them the picture of a tempestuous sea, into which sinners have already fallen from the ship of divine grace; they are already dashed about on every side by remorse of conscience and by fear of the judgments of God; they are without light or guide and are at the point of losing the last breath of hope and falling into despair; then it is that our Lord, pointing out Mary to them, who is often called "Star of the Sea," raises His voice and says:

"O poor lost sinners, despair not; raise up your eyes and look at this beautiful star; breathe again with confidence, for it will save you from this tempest, and will guide you into the port of salvation."

St. Bernard says the same thing: "If you would not be lost in the storm, look on the star, call upon Mary!"

Isaiah complained of the times in which he lived: "Behold, you are angry because we have sinned . . . there is none . . . who rises up and takes hold of you." (64:5) St. Bonaventure in commenting on that passage says: "It is true, Lord, that at the time there was no one to raise up sinners and hold back your wrath, for Mary was not yet born; before Mary there was no one who would dare to intercede to restrain the avenging arm of God."

This Mother of mercy has so great a desire to save the most abandoned sinners that she herself goes in search of them, in order to help them. If they have recourse to her, she knows how to find the means to render them acceptable to God.

St. Bridget once heard Jesus Christ address His Mother in this way: "You would be ready to obtain the grace of God for Lucifer himself, if only he humbled himself so far as to seek your aid." That proud spirit will never humble himself so far as to implore the protection of Mary; but if such a thing were possible, Mary would be sufficiently compassionate, and her prayers would have sufficient power to obtain both forgiveness and salvation for him from God.

Noah's ark was a true figure of Mary, for as in it all kinds of beasts were saved, so under the mantle of Mary all sinners, who by their vices are already like beasts, find refuge. There is this difference: the brutes that entered the ark remained brutes, the wolf remaining a wolf, the tiger remaining a tiger — but under the mantle of Mary, the wolf becomes a lamb, and the tiger a dove.

It is related in the Scriptures that Boaz allowed Ruth "to gather the ears of corn after the reapers." (Ruth 2:2) St. Bonaventure says that: "As Ruth found favor with Boaz, so Mary has found favor with our Lord and is also allowed to gather the ears of corn after the reapers. The reapers followed by Mary are all evangelical laborers, missionaries, preachers and confessors who are constantly reaping souls for God. But there are some hardened and rebellious souls which are abandoned even by these. To Mary alone it is granted to save them by her powerful intercession."

With reason, then, did St. John Damascene salute her as the "hope of those who are in despair." With reason, St. Lawrence Justinian calls her "the hope of malefactors." St. Ephrem calls her "the safe harbor of all sailing on the sea of the world." And St. Bernard exults: "Who, O Lady, can be without confidence in you, since you assist even those who are in despair!"

## PRAYER

*May God be eternally blessed and thanked, for having created Mary so amiable and benign, even towards the most miserable of sinners! Truly unfortunate is he who does not love you, Mary, and who, having it in his power to obtain your assistance, has lost confidence in you.*

*Who was ever lost that had recourse to the most Blessed
Virgin!*

*Abandon me not, my Mother. Never, never cease to pray for
me until you see me safe in heaven at your feet, blessing and
thanking you forever, in Christ, our Lord.    Amen.*

# CHAPTER IV

# AD TE CLAMAMUS, EXSULES FILII EVAE

*To You We Cry, Poor Banished Children of Eve*

*i*

**MARY OUR HELP.**

The promptness of Mary in assisting those who invoke her.

We poor children of Eve are truly unfortunate; for, guilty of her fault, and condemned to the same penalty, we have to wander about in this valley of tears as exiles from our country, and to weep over our many afflictions of body and soul.

But blessed is the person who, in the midst of these sorrows, often turns to the comfortress of this world, to the refuge of the unfortunate, to the great Mother of God, and devoutly calls on her and invokes her.

"Blessed is the one that hears me, and that watches daily at my gates." (Prov 8:34) Blessed, says Mary, is the one who listens to my counsel, and watches continually at the gate of my mercy, and invokes my intercession and aid.

Holy Church carefully teaches us, her children, with what attention and confidence we should unceasingly have recourse to this loving protectress. The Church has instituted many festivals that are celebrated throughout the year in honor of this great Queen.

She also puts aside Saturday each week to honor Mary; in the Office, the Liturgy of the Word, there is the daily invocation of the name of Mary; and we are invited to salute Mary three times a day in the Angelus. Holy Church also promotes the Rosary, novenas, processions and visits to shrines of the Blessed Mother.

And all of this is pleasing to Mary, not that she needs our devotion, but that as we open ourselves to her, she is able to do even more for us, her children.

And how prompt is this good Mother in responding to all who call upon her! Even so simple a prayer as the Hail Mary will draw her immediate attention. In the exercise of her mercy she does not know how to act differently from God. As He flies at once to the assistance of those who beg His aid, faithful to His promise, "Ask and you shall receive" (Jn 16:24), so Mary, whenever she is invoked, is at once ready to assist those who pray to her.

This will explain a passage in the Gospel of St. Luke, in which we are told that when Mary went to visit and shower graces on St. Elizabeth and her whole family, she was not slow, but she went with speed. The Gospel says: "And Mary, rising up, went with haste into the hill country." (1:39) And this is not said of her return to Nazareth.

Nor should the multitude of our sins diminish our confidence that Mary will grant our petitions when we cast ourselves before her. She is the Mother of mercy, but mercy would not be needed if no one existed who required it. Just as a good mother does not shrink from applying a remedy to a sick child, no matter the nature or character of the illness, so our good Mother is unable to abandon us when we have recourse to her, that she may heal the wounds caused by our sins, no matter how loathsome they may be.

This good Mother's compassion is so great that she does not even wait for our prayers in order to assist us, but as is expressed in the Book of Wisdom, "She hastens to make herself known in anticipation of men's desire." (6:13) St. Anselm applies these words to her, saying that she anticipates those who desire her protection.

Mary, even when living in this world, showed at the marriage feast of Cana, the great compassion that she would afterwards exercise towards us in our necessities. It is as if these needs force her to take pity on us and assist us, even before we ask her.

In the second chapter of St. John we read that at this feast the compassionate Mother saw the embarrassment in which the bride and bridegroom were, and that they were quite ashamed on seeing the wine fail. Without being asked, and listening only to the dictates of her loving heart, which could never see the afflictions of others without feeling for them, she begged her Son to console them simply by laying their distress before Him: "They have no wine." (2:3)

No sooner had she done this than our Lord, in order to satisfy all present, and still more to console the compassionate heart of His Mother, who had asked the favor, worked the well-known miracle by which He changed the water brought to Him in jars into wine.

If Mary, thus unasked, is so prompt to help the needy, how much more will she come to the rescue of those who do ask her? Should there be anyone who doubts as to whether Mary will come to his aid, Pope Innocent III remarks: "Who is there that ever, when in the night of sin, had recourse to this dear Lady without being relieved?"

"I am satisfied," says St. Bernard, "that whoever has recourse to you, O Blessed Virgin, in his wants, and can remember that he did so in vain, should no more speak of or praise your mercy." Sooner would heaven and earth be destroyed than would Mary fail to assist anyone who asks her for help, provided he does so with a good intention and with confidence in her.

St Anselm reminds us that we may obtain mercy more quickly from Mary than from Jesus, because Jesus is also a judge who can punish, while Mary exercises mercy as a patroness. It is not as if Mary were more powerful than Jesus, for we know that Jesus Christ is our only Savior, and that He alone by His merits has obtained and obtains salvation for us.

He reminds us: "We often obtain more promptly what we ask by invoking Mary than by invoking Jesus. Her Son is lord and judge of all, and discerns the merits of each one; therefore, if He does not immediately grant the prayers of all, He is just. When however, the Mother's name is invoked, though the merits of the suppliant are not such as to deserve that his favor be granted, those of the Mother supply, that he may receive."

Many things are asked from God and are not granted; they are asked from Mary and are obtained. Now why is this? Because God has thus decreed to honor His Mother.

In the 50th chapter of the first book of her revelations, St. Bridget heard Jesus address His Mother in this way: "You shall present me with no petition that will be refused. My Mother, ask whatever you will, for never will I refuse you anything. Know also, that I promise graciously to hear all who ask any favor from me in your name though they may be sinners, if only they have the will to amend their lives."

The same thing was revealed to St. Gertrude when she heard our divine Redeemer assure His Mother that in His omnipotence He granted her power to show mercy to sinners who invoked her name in whatever manner she might please.

## *PRAYER*
### (attributed to St. Bernard)

*Remember O most gracious Virgin Mary, that never was it known, that anyone who fled to your protection, implored your help, or sought your intercession, was left unaided. Inspired by this confidence, we fly unto you, O Virgin of Virgins, our mother. To you do we come, before you we kneel, sinful and sorrowful. O Mother of the Word Incarnate, despise not our petitions, but in your clemency, hear and answer us.     Amen.*

## *ii*

### THE GREATNESS OF THE POWER OF MARY TO DEFEND THOSE WHO INVOKE HER WHEN TEMPTED BY THE DEVIL

Not only is the most Blessed Virgin Queen of heaven and of all the saints, but she is also Queen of hell and all evil spirits: she overcame them valiantly by her virtue. From the very beginning God foretold the victory and empire that our Queen would one day obtain over the serpent, when he announced that a woman should come into the world to conquer him: "I will put enmities between you and the woman. . . ." (Gen 3:15)

Who could this woman be but Mary, who by her fair humility and holy life always conquered him and beat down his strength? The Mother of our Lord Jesus Christ was promised in the person of that woman, as St. Cyprian remarks, for God did not say "I place enmities," as if to refer to Eve, but "I will place" to point to Mary in the future.

The Septuagint says, "And he will crush your head," while the Vulgate version has it, "she will crush your head." This is the sense known by St. Ambrose, St. Jerome, St. Augustine, and a great many others.

However, it really does not matter, whether the Mother crushes the head of the serpent through her Son, or the Son overcomes Lucifer through His Mother who brought Him into the world to effect this. As St. Bernard remarks, this proud spirit, in spite of himself, was beaten down and trampled under foot by this most Blessed Virgin. As a slave conquered in war, the devil is forced to obey the commands of this Queen.

St. Bruno quotes the common thought of the saints when he says "that Eve was the cause of death," by allowing herself to be overcome by the serpent, "but that Mary," by conquering the devil, "restored life to us."

In ancient Judea, victories were gained by means of the ark. Thus it was that Moses conquered his enemies as we learn from the Book of Numbers: "And when the ark was lifted up, Moses said, 'Arise. O Lord, and let your enemies be scattered.'" (10:35) Thus was Jericho conquered; thus also the Philistines; "for the ark of God was there." (1 Sam 14:18)

It is well known that the ark was a figure of Mary. Manna was kept in the ark, and so Jesus, of whom the manna was a figure, in Mary. By means of this ark we gain victory over our earthly and infernal enemies. "And thus," St. Bernardine of Siena well observes, "when Mary, the ark of the New Testament, was raised to the dignity of Queen of Heaven, the power of hell over men was weakened and dissolved."

O how the infernal spirits tremble at the very thought of Mary, and of her august name! St. Bonaventure points out: "O how fearful is Mary to the devils." He compares these enemies to those of whom Job speaks: "In the night the thief roams, and he puts a mask over his face; in the dark he breaks into houses." (24:15-16)

Thieves go and rob houses in the dark; but as soon as morning dawns, they fly as if they could see the shadows of death. "It is precisely this that the devils do," says this saint; "they enter a soul in time of darkness," meaning when the soul is in the grasp of ignorance. They dig through the house of our mind when it is in the darkness of ignorance.

But then he adds: "If suddenly they are overtaken by the dawn, that is, if grace and the mercy of Mary enters the soul, its brightness instantly dispels the darkness and puts the infernal enemies to flight, as if they fled from death." O blessed is the one who invokes Mary in his conflicts with hell!

In confirmation of this it was revealed to St. Bridget: "That God has rendered Mary so powerful over the devils, that as often as they assault a devout client who calls upon Mary for help, she at a single glance instantly terrifies them, so that they fly far away, preferring to have their pains redoubled rather than see themselves subject to the power of Mary."

St. John Damascene used to say: "While I keep my hope in you intact, O Mother of God, I shall be safe. I will fight and overcome my enemies with no other buckler than your protection and your all-powerful intercession." All who are so fortunate as to be clients of this great Queen can say the same thing. St. James the Monk adds: "You, O Lord, have given us in Mary arms that no force of spiritual warfare can overcome, and a trophy never to be destroyed."

It is said in the Old Testament, that God guided His people from Egypt to the land of promise "by day in a column of cloud, and by night in a column of fire." (Ex 13:21) Some spiritual writers apply this to Mary in her two-fold function towards her people. As a cloud she protects us from the ardor of divine justice; as a fire she protects us from the devils.

So Bonaventure comments: "As wax melts before the fire, so do the devils lose their power against those souls who remember the name of Mary and devoutly invoke it; and still more so if they endeavor to imitate her virtues."

St. Bernard declares that: "The devils not only fear, but tremble at the very sound of Mary's name." Thomas a Kempis expresses the same sentiment: "The evil spirits greatly fear the Queen of heaven, and fly at the sound of her name, as if from fire. At the very sound of the word Mary, they are prostrated as by thunder."

O how many victories have the clients of Mary gained by making use of her most holy name! In this St. Anthony of Padua was always victorious. Blessed Henry Suso testifies to the same thing, as does St. Anselm. We have also had stories coming from the missions to Japan that witness this truth.

"You, O Lady," says St. Germanus, "by the simple invocation of your most powerful name, give security to your servants against all the assaults of the enemy." Blessed Allan adds: "At the very sound of these words, 'Hail, Mary!' Satan flies and hell trembles."

Our Blessed Lady revealed to St. Bridget that the enemy flees even from the most abandoned sinners, and who consequently are the farthest from God, and fully possessed by the devil, if they only invoke her most powerful name with a true purpose of amendment. At the same time, our Blessed Lady added: "That if the soul does not amend and obliterate its sins by sorrow, the devils return almost immediately and continue to possess it."

# PRAYER

*Behold at your feet, O Mary, a poor sinner who has so many times, by his own fault, been a slave of hell. I know that by neglecting to have recourse to you, my refuge, I allowed myself to be overcome by the devil.*

*Had I always had recourse to you, had I always invoked your name, I certainly should not have fallen. Ah, my Queen and my refuge, assist me. Place me under your mantle of mercy and do not let me fall again into the power of hell.*

*When my last struggle with hell comes at the moment of my death, help me more than ever. Fill me with the confidence that will enable me to expire with the sweet names of Jesus and Mary on my lips.     Amen.*

# CHAPTER V

# AD TE SUSPIRAMUS GEMENTES ET FLENTES IN HAC LACRYMARUM VALLE

*To You Do We Sigh, Mourning and Weeping in this Valley of Tears*

## *i*

### MARY, OUR MEDIATRIX: THE NECESSITY OF THE INTERCESSION OF MARY FOR OUR SALVATION

That it is not only lawful but useful to invoke and pray to the saints, and more especially to the Queen of the saints, the most holy and ever blessed Virgin Mary, in order that they may obtain for us the divine grace, is an article of faith, and has been defined by general Councils.

This refutes heretics who condemned it as injurious to Jesus Christ, who is our only mediator. But if a Jeremiah after his death prayed for Jerusalem (2 Macc 15:14), if the ancients of the Book of Revelation presented the prayers of the saints to God (Rev 5:8), if a St. Peter promises his disciples that after his death he will be mindful of them (2 P 1:15), if a holy Stephen prays for his persecutors (Ac 7:59), if a St. Paul prays for his companions (Ac 27:24; Ep 2:16; Ph 1:4; Col 1:3); if, in fine, the saints can pray for us, why can we not ask the saints to intercede for us?

St. Paul recommends himself to the prayers of his disciples: "Brothers, pray for us." (1 Th 5:25) St. James exhorts us to pray for one another: "Pray for one another, that you may be saved." (Jm 5:16)

No one denies that Jesus Christ is our only mediator of justice, and that He by His merits has obtained our reconciliation with God. But, on the other hand, it is impious to assert that God is not pleased to grant graces at the intercession of His saints, and more especially of Mary His Mother, whom Jesus desires so much to see loved and honored by all.

Who can pretend that the honor bestowed on a mother does not redound to the honor of the son? "The glory of children are their fathers." (Prov 17:6) Therefore St. Bernard says: "Let us not imagine that we obscure the glory of the Son by the great praise we lavish on the Mother; for the more she is honored, the greater is the glory of the Son."

"There can be no doubt," he adds, "that whatever we say in praise of the Mother is equally in praise of the Son." St. Ildephonsus also says: "That which is given to the Mother redounds to the Son; the honor given to the Queen is honor bestowed on the King."

There can be no doubt that by the merits of Jesus, Mary was made the mediatrix of our salvation — not, indeed, a mediatrix of justice, but of favor and intercession. St. Bonaventure expressly calls her: "Mary, the most faithful mediatrix of our salvation." St. Lawrence Justinian asks: "How can she be otherwise than full of grace, who has been made the ladder to paradise, the gate of heaven, the most true mediatrix between God and man?"

According to the learned theologian Suarez, if we implore

our Blessed Lady to obtain a favor for us, it is not because we distrust the divine mercy, but rather that we fear our own unworthiness and the absence of proper dispositions. We recommend ourselves to Mary, that her dignity may supply for our lowliness.

We apply to Mary in order that the dignity of the intercessor may supply for our misery. So, to invoke the aid of the most Blessed Virgin is not diffidence in the divine mercy, but dread of our own unworthiness.

That it is most useful and holy to have recourse to the intercession of Mary can only be doubted by those who have not faith. But, what we intend to prove here, is that the intercession of Mary is even necessary to salvation. We say necessary — not absolutely but morally.

This necessity proceeds from the will itself of God, that all the graces that He dispenses should pass through the hands of Mary, according to the opinion of St. Bernard, and which we may now with safety call the general opinion of theologians and learned writers. Or as St. Bernard puts it: "Such is God's will, that we should have all through Mary."

Does this sound like hyperbole, the exggerated language of love? Let me repeat, the mediation of justice by way of merit is one thing, reserved to Jesus Christ alone; mediation by way of prayer is another.

Again, it is one thing to say that God cannot, and another to say that He will not, grant graces without the intercession of Mary. We willingly admit that God is the source of every good, and the absolute master of all graces. Mary is only a pure creature who receives whatever she obtains as a pure favor from God.

Therefore, it seems reasonable to me to assert that God, in order to exult this great creature, who more than all others honored and loved Him during her life, and whom, moreover, He had chosen to be the Mother of his Son, our common

Redeemer, wills that all graces that are granted to those whom He has redeemed should pass through and be dispensed by the hands of Mary.

We most readily admit that Jesus Christ is the only Mediator of justice, according to the distinction just made, and that by His merits He obtains for us all the graces and salvation. We also say that Mary is the Mediatrix of grace, and that receiving all she obtains through Jesus Christ, and because she prays and asks for it in the name of Jesus Christ, yet all the same whatever graces we receive, they come to us through her intercession.

This seems quite in accordance with the sentiments of holy Church in its public and approved prayers in which we are continually taught to have recourse to this great Mother, and to invoke her as "health of the weak, refuge of sinners, the help of Christians, and as our life and hope."

If we fear excess in praising Mary, listen to the words of St. Augustine, for he declares that whatever we may say in praise of Mary is little in comparison with that which she deserves on account of her dignity as Mother of God. Moreover, the Church says, in the Mass appointed for her festivals: "You are happy, O most holy Virgin Mary, and most worthy of all praise."

See what the saints have to say on this point. St. Bernard says that: "God has filled Mary with all the graces, so that men may receive by her means, as by a channel, every good thing that comes to them. She is a full aqueduct, that others may receive of her fullness." Heavenly graces flow through her.

St. Antoninus teaches that: "All the graces that have ever been bestowed on mankind, all came through Mary." St. Bonaventure states: "As the moon, which stands between the sun and the earth, transmits to this latter whatever it receives from the former, so does Mary pour out upon us who are in this world the heavenly graces that she receives from the divine sun of justice."

Saints like Sophronius and Bernardine of Siena remind us that Christ is the head of the mystical body and Mary is, as it were, the neck through which the life-giving graces flow down into the body.

It is almost impossible to number the saints and spiritual writers who favor this proposition, that the graces of God come through the mediation of Mary. This mediation is not only useful, but necessary. Necessary, in accordance with what we have already said, not with an absolute necessity. The mediation of Jesus Christ alone is of absolute necessity. We are speaking here of a moral necessity, for the Church believes with St. Bernard, that God has determined that no grace shall be granted otherwise than by the hands of Mary. Indeed, God did not become man without the consent of Mary.

St. Bonaventure, in his sermon on the Epiphany, notes the words, "They found the Child with Mary his Mother" (Mt 2:11), and reminds us that if we wish to find Jesus we must go through Mary. It is vain to look for Jesus unless we try to do so through Mary. Or as St. Ildephonsus reasons: "I desire to be the servant of the Son, but because no one will ever be so without serving Mary, for this reason I desire to be a servant of Mary."

# PRAYER

*O my soul, see what a sure hope of salvation and eternal life our Lord has given you, by having in His mercy inspired you with such confidence in the patronage of His Mother.*

*Thank God for this mercy, and thank the Blessed Mother who has condescended to take you under her mantle. O yes, I thank you, most loving Mother, for all the grace you have obtained for me. From how many dangers you have delivered me!*

*How many favors and inspirations you have given me! How often you have helped me return to the favor of God! There is so much I owe you for your kindness to me.*

*Now you ask me to love your God. I ask you to obtain this precious gift of loving God, so that I may love and serve Him forever. Amen*


## ii

### THE SAME SUBJECT CONTINUED

St. Bernard says: "That as a man and a woman cooperated in our ruin, so it was proper that another man and another woman should cooperate in our redemption, and these two were Jesus and his Mother, Mary. There is no doubt that Jesus Christ alone was more than sufficient to redeem us; but it was more becoming that both sexes should cooperate in the reparation of an evil in which both shared the cause."

St. Albert the Great calls Mary the "helper of redemption." The Blessed Virgin revealed to St. Bridget that: "As Adam and Eve sold the world for an apple, so did she with her Son redeem it, as it were, with one heart." St. Anselm adds: "That although God could create the world out of nothing yet, when it was lost by sin, He would not repair the evil without the cooperation of Mary."

Suarez writes that: "Mary cooperated in our salvation in three ways: first, by having merited, by a merit of congruity, the Incarnation of the Word; second, by having continually prayed for us while she was living in this world; third, by having willingly sacrificed the life of her Son to God."

For this reason our Lord has justly decreed, that as Mary cooperated in the salvation of mankind with so much love, and at the same time gave such glory to God, so all men through her intercession are to obtain their salvation.

St. Elizabeth told Mary: "Blessed are you among women and blessed is the fruit of your womb." (Lk 1:42) Whoever, therefore, desires the fruit must go to the tree; whoever desires Jesus must go to Mary; and whoever finds Mary will most certainly find Jesus.

When St. Elizabeth saw that the most Blessed Virgin had come to visit her in her own home, not knowing how to thank her, and filled with humility, she exclaimed: "And how is it that the Mother of my Lord should come to me?" (Lk 1:43)

Elizabeth knew that Jesus entered her home with Mary, as is always the case. When Mary arrives she brings Jesus. Therefore it was sufficient to thank the Mother without naming the Son.

Another author objects that we cannot ask Mary to save us since this belongs to God alone. But since a culprit condemned to death can beg a royal favorite to save him by interceding with the king that his life may be spared, why cannot we ask the Mother of God to save us by obtaining eternal life for us?

St. John Damascene did not scruple to cry out: "Pure and immaculate Virgin, save me, and deliver me from eternal damnation!" St. Bonaventure called Mary "the salvation of those who invoked her." And St. Germanus had written previously: "No one is saved but through Mary."

St. Cajetan used to say that we may seek for graces but shall never find them without the intercession of Mary. St. Antoninus expresses it this way: "Whoever asks and expects to obtain graces without the intercession of Mary endeavors to fly without wings."

Blessed Raymond Jordan repeats the same thing: "Our salvation is in her hands." Cassian is even stronger, saying: "The salvation of all depends on their being favored and protected by Mary."

And as we have access to the Eternal Father, says St. Bernard, only through Jesus Christ, so have we access to Jesus Christ only through Mary: "By you we have access to the Son, O blessed finder of grace, bearer of life, and mother of salvation, that we may receive Him from you, who through you was given to us."

This is the reason given by the same saint why our Lord has determined that all shall be saved by the intercession of Mary, and therefore he calls her the Mother of Grace and of our salvation.

But, our objecting author continues: "If all graces come through Mary, then it is useless to have recourse to any of the other saints." What difficulty can there be in saying that God, in order to honor His Mother, and having made her the Queen of the Saints, and willing that all graces shall be dispensed by her, should also will that the saints address themselves to her to obtain favors for their clients?

I find that St. Bernard, St. Anselm, St. Bonaventure, Suarez and many noted authors express this thought. For example, St. Bernard writes: "In vain would a person ask other saints for a favor, if Mary did not interpose to obtain it." And this is precisely what St. Benedict promised St. Frances of Rome, for he appeared to her, and taking her under his protection, he promised that he would be her advocate with the Mother of God.

And so, finally, we can understand why holy Church encourages us to salute Mary as "our hope." It is indeed a glorious title. God alone is the source of all good, and Jesus Christ is the sole and unique Mediator between God and man. But since God wills that Mary, herself a mere creature and so dependent on God, but also the fairest creature of our race, be the representative of mankind, the mediation of Christ is actually poured into the world, channeled through her.

\*   \*   \*   \*   \*   \*   \*   \*   \*   \*

*Editorial Note*:   In his encyclical, **Redemptoris Mater**, March 25, 1987, Pope John Paul II speaks of Mary as Mediatrix in at least six places. In his encyclical he comments extensively on the Marian passages in the documents of the Second Vatican Council and includes passages from previous Popes, and passages often quoted in this work by St. Alphonsus.

Thus: Paragraph 40 *Redemptoris Mater*: "With the redeeming death of her son, the maternal mediation of the handmaid of the Lord took on a universal dimension, for the work of redemption embraces the whole of humanity . . . Mary's motherhood continues unceasingly in the Church as the mediation which interceded, and the Church expresses her faith in this truth by invoking Mary under the titles of Advocate, Auxiliatrix, Adjutrix and Mediatrix."

Paragraph 38: "The Church knows and teaches with St. Paul that there is only one mediator: 'For there is one God, and there is one mediator between God and men, the man Christ Jesus, who gave himself as ransom for all.' (1 Tm 2:50-6) 'The maternal role of Mary towards people in no way obscures or diminishes the unique mediation of Christ, but rather shows its power.' (*Lumen Gentium* 60): it is a mediation in Christ."

"The Church knows and teaches that 'all the saving influences of the Blessed Virgin on mankind originate . . . from the divine pleasure. They flow forth from the superabundance of the merits of Christ, rest on his mediation, depend entirely on it, and draw all their power from it. In no way do they impede the immediate union of the faithful with Christ. Rather, they foster this union.' (*Lumen Gentium* 60)"

# PRAYER

*O loving Mother of the redeemer,*
*gate of heaven, star of the sea,*
*assist your people who have fallen yet strive to rise again.*
*To the wonderment of nature you bore your Creator,*
*yet remained a virgin after as before.*
*You who received Gabriel's joyful greeting*
*have pity on us poor sinners.*

* *Alma Redemptoris Mater* attributed to Hermanus Contractus.

# CHAPTER VI

# EIA ERGO, ADVOCATA NOSTRA!
## A Gracious Advocate

### i

**MARY OUR ADVOCATE: MARY IS AN ADVOCATE WHO IS ABLE TO SAVE ALL.**

So great is the authority that mothers possess over their sons, that even if they are monarchs, and have absolute dominion over every person in their kingdom, yet never can mothers become subjects of their sons. It is true that Jesus now in heaven sits at the right hand of the Father, that is, as St. Thomas Aquinas explains it, even as man, on account of the hypostatical union with the person of the Divine Word.

He has supreme dominion over all, and also over Mary. Nevertheless, it will always be true that for a time, when He was living in this world, He was pleased to humble Himself and to be subject to Mary, as we are told by St. Luke: "And He was subject to them." (2:51) And still, more, says St. Ambrose, Jesus Christ, having deigned to make Mary His Mother, inasmuch as He was her Son, He was truly obliged to obey her.

Now in heaven, Mary can no longer command her Son; nevertheless her prayers are always the prayers of the Mother, and consequently most powerful to obtain whatever she asks. As St. Bonaventure remarks: "Mary has this great privilege that with her Son she above all the saints is most powerful to obtain whatever she wills." And why? Precisely because they are the prayers of a mother.

According to St. Peter Damian: "All power is given to you in heaven and on earth and nothing is impossible to you who can even raise those who are in despair to the hope of salvation." And then he adds: "When the Mother goes to seek a favor for us from Jesus Christ" (whom the saint calls the golden altar of mercy at which sinners obtain pardon), "her Son esteems her prayers so greatly, and is so desirous to satisfy her, that when she prays it seems as if she commanded rather than prayed, and was rather a Queen than a handmaid."

St. Bernardine does not fear to utter this sentence: "At the command of Mary all obey, even God!" He means that God grants the prayers of Mary as if they were commands. St. Anselm, addressing Mary says: "Our Lord, O most holy Virgin, has exalted you to such a degree that by His favor all things that are possible to Him should be possible to you."

That Mary is willing to use her powerful intercession for all is expressed by St. Bernard in this way: "The most powerful and merciful charity of the Mother of God abounds in tender compassion and in effectual help. It is equally rich in both."

From the time that Mary came into the world her only thought, after seeking the glory of God, was to help the miserable. Even then she enjoyed the privilege of obtaining whatever she wished. This we see from the powerful miracle Christ worked at her request at the marriage feast in Cana.

So confident was Mary in her privilege that, even though Christ seemed to demur, she turned to the servants and acted as if the request had already been granted. To honor His Mother, our Lord anticipated the time for the working of miracles.

In fine, it is certain that no creature can obtain so many mercies for us as this tender advocate who is so honored by God, not only as His beloved handmaid, but also as His true Mother. Mary has only to speak and her Son executes all. How does Mary obtain such favors? She has only to let her voice be heard and her Son immediately grants her prayer.

Valerius Maximus relates that when Coriolanus was besieging Rome, he would not listen to the requests of his friends and the citizens to cease. But as soon as he saw his mother, Veturia, imploring him, he could no longer refuse, and immediately raised the siege. Certainly the prayers of Mary with Jesus are as much more powerful than those of Veturia, as the love and gratitude of this Son for His most dear Mother are greater.

This was acknowledged by the devil himself to St. Dominic who had obliged him to speak by the mouth of a possessed person. He said: "A single sigh from Mary was worth more before God than the united prayers of all the saints."

St. Bridget heard the saints in heaven addressing our Lady in this way: "O most blessed Queen, what is there that you cannot accomplish? You have only to will it and it is accomplished." St. George of Nicomedia explains it in this manner: Jesus Christ, as if it were to satisfy an obligation under which He placed Himself towards His Mother, when she consented to give Him His human nature, grants all she asks. "The Son, as if paying a debt, grants all your petitions."

The martyr St. Methodius exclaims: "Rejoice, rejoice, O Mary, for you have your Son for a debtor, who gives to all and receives from none. We are all God's debtors for all that we possess, for all is His gift. But God has been pleased to become your debtor in taking flesh from you and becoming man."

St. Augustine says that Mary gave flesh to the divine Word

so that he could supply the price of our redemption that we might be delivered from eternal death: "Therefore, she is more powerful than all others to help us gain eternal life."

St. Theophilus of Alexandria, who lived in the time of St. Jerome, left this note in writing: "The prayers of His Mother are a pleasure to the Son because He desires to grant all that is granted on her account and so recompense her for the favor she did Him in giving Him His body."

And St. John Damascene, addressing the Blessed Virgin, said: "You, O Mary, being Mother of the most high God, can save all by your prayers which are increased in value by the maternal authority."

Let us conclude with St. Bonaventure who, considering the benefit conferred on us by our Lord in giving us Mary for our advocate, addresses her in this manner: "O truly immense and admirable goodness of our God, which has been pleased to grant you, O sovereign Mother, to us miserable sinners for our advocate, in order that you, by your powerful intercession, may obtain all that you please for us."

He continues: "O wonderful mercy of our God, who, in order that we might not die on account of the sentence that might be pronounced against us, has given us His own Mother and the patroness of graces to be our advocate."

## PRAYER

*I will address you, O great Mother of God, in the words of St. Bernard: "Speak, O Lady for your Son hears you, and whatever you ask you will obtain." Speak, speak, then O Mary, our advocate, in favor of us poor miserable sinners.*

*Remember that it was also for our good that you received so much power and so high a dignity. The Son of God was*

*pleased to take His humanity from you so that you might
dispense the riches of divine mercy to all sinners. He won these
mercies for us at so great a price!*

*We may be great sinners, but God has enriched you with
compassion and power far exceeding our iniquities. Obtain for
us true conversion; obtain for us the love of God, the gift of
perseverance and help us come home to you in heaven at last,
where we may enjoy the presence of your Son, our Redeemer.
Amen.*

## *ii*

### MARY IS SO TENDER AN ADVOCATE THAT SHE
### DOES NOT REFUSE TO DEFEND THE CAUSE EVEN OF
### THE MOST MISERABLE

So many are the reasons that we have for loving this most loving
Queen, that if Mary was praised throughout the world; if in
every sermon Mary alone was spoken of; if all gave their lives for
Mary; still all would be little in comparison with the homage and
gratitude that we owe her in return for the tender love she bears
for all, and even to the most miserable sinners who preserve even
the slightest spark of devotion for her.

All of this human praise would be as nothing compared to
the praise God has given her by the singular honor of choosing
her to be the Mother of God!

Blessed Raymond Jordan makes a point of Mary's regard
for the welfare of sinners: "Her kindness and mercy are so great,
that no one, however enormous his sins may be, should fear to
cast himself at her feet. She can never reject anyone who has
recourse to her."

He continues: "Mary, as our most loving advocate, herself
offers the prayers of her servants to God, and especially those

who place themselves in her hands. As the Son intercedes for us with the Father, so she intercedes for us with the Son. She works to obtain the great affair of our salvation and to gain us the graces we ask."

With good reason, then, does Denis the Carthusian call the Blessed Virgin, "the singular refuge of the lost, the hope of the most abandoned, and the advocate of all sinners who have recourse to her."

But suppose there is a sinner who knows of her power but who doubts her compassion, feeling that his sins are too great. St. Bonaventure hastens to reassure him: "the great, the special privilege of Mary is that she is all-powerful with her Son. Why does she have such power, if not to care for us sinners? Let us thank God that He has made her such a powerful patron and that she exercises her power in behalf of all sinners, whatever their deeds."

"And who, O Mother of mercy," exclaims St. Germanus, in the joy of his heart, "who, after your own Jesus, is as tenderly solicitous for our welfare as you are? Who defends us in times of temptation as you do? Who undertakes to protect sinners and fight for them as you do? Your patronage, O Mary, is more powerful and loving than anything of which we can form an idea."

Mary takes care of all, even of sinners. Indeed she glories in being called in a special sense their advocate, as she declares to Venerable Mary Villani, saying: "After the title of Mother of God, I rejoice most in that of advocate of sinners."

St. Amadeus says that: "Our Queen is constantly before the divine Majesty, interceding for us with her most powerful prayers. She well knows our miseries, and she constantly shows a meternal care and love for us. She is always praying for us to help us work out our salvation."

"O with what efficacy and love does this good advocate interest herself in the affair of our salvation," says St. Bernard. St.

Bonaventure praises her for the great zeal she has to ask the Lord to pardon our sins, help us with His grace and free us from dangers.

Truly unfortunate should we poor sinners be, had we not this great advocate who is so powerful and so compassionate, and at the same time so prudent and wise that the great Judge, her Son, cannot condemn the guilty who are defended by her. St. John Geometra salutes her, saying: "Hail, O court, for putting an end to litigation."

St. Bonaventure called Mary, "the wise Abigail." This is the woman in the Book of Samuel (1 Sm 15) who, by her wise supplications, knew so well how to appease King David when he was indignant against her husband, Nabal. She even induced David to bless her in gratitude for having prevented him from avenging himself on Nabal with excessive violence. This, indeed, is what Mary does for us in heaven at the throne of her Son, appeasing the divine justice.

"It was on this account," says St. Bernard, "that the Eternal Father, wishing to show all the mercy possible, besides giving us Jesus Christ as our principal advocate, was also pleased to give us Mary as our special advocate with Jesus Christ."

"There is no doubt," he adds, "that Jesus Christ is the only mediator of justice between God and mankind. By virtue of His own merits and promises, He will and can obtain for us pardon and all the divine favors. But because men acknowledge and fear the divine Majesty and the terrible justice, we have been given Mary as an advocate with Jesus to allay our fears and give us more confidence."

Read all that the Gospels have to say about Mary and you will find no strain of severity. Therefore, go to her with joyful hearts and entrust yourself to her intercession.

"Be comfortable then, O you who fear," I will say with St. Thomas of Villanova: "breath freely and take courage. O wretched sinners; this great Virgin, who is the Mother of your God and judge us also the advocate of the whole human race; fit for this office, for she does what she wills with God; most wise, for she knows all the means of appeasing Him; universal, for she welcome all and refuses to defend no one."

## *PRAYER*
## William of Paris

*O most glorious Mother of God, I, in the miserable state to which I am reduced by my sins, have recourse to you, full of confidence. The whole Church of the faithful rejoices to call and proclaim you the Mother of mercy.*

*You, O Mary, so dear to God, are always willing to listen to us. You have never despised a contrite sinner. Never, O my Mother, let my sins prevent me from coming to you to benefit from your charity.*

*You are our advocate, the mediatrix of peace between God and man. After your Son, you are our only hope and the secure refuge of the miserable. The divine Word became man to save sinners, and He became man through your humanity. You are, therefore, at the heart of His plan for our salvation.*

*You brought the very source of tender compassion into the world, your Son Jesus Christ. Far be it from you not to share in His plan. Let your tender compassion, which far exceeds my sins, move you to help me.    Amen.*

## *iii*

### MARY IS THE PEACE-MAKER BETWEEN
### SINNERS AND GOD

The grace of God is the greatest and the most desirable of treasures for every soul. It is called by the Holy Spirit an infinite treasure; for by means of divine grace we are raised to the honor of being the friends of God. Jesus Christ, our Redeemer and God, did not hesitate to call those His friends who were in grace: "You are my friends." (Jn 15:14)

O accursed sin that dissolves this friendship! "But your sins," says the prophet Isaiah, "have put a division between you and your God. (59:2) And putting hatred between the soul and God, it is changed from a friend into an enemy of its Lord, as expressed in the Book of Wisdom: "But to God the wicked and his wickedness are hateful alike." (14:9)

What then, must a sinner do who has the misfortune to be the enemy of God? He must find a mediator who will obtain pardon for him and who will enable him to recover the lost friendship of God.

"Be comforted, O unfortunate soul, who has lost your God," says St. Bernard: "Your Lord has provided you with a mediator, and it is His Son Jesus who can obtain for you all that you desire. He has given you Jesus for a mediator; and what is there that such a Son cannot obtain from the Father?"

But, St. Bernard asks, why should this merciful Savior, who gave His life to save us, ever be thought of as severe? Why should people believe Him terrible, who is all love? O distrustful sinners, what do you fear?

If your fear arises from having offended God, you know that Jesus had fastened all your sins to the Cross with His own lacerated hands, and having satisfied divine justice for them by His death, He has already effaced them from your souls.

Here are that saint's own words: "They imagine Him rigorous, who is all compassion; terrible, who is love. What do you fear, O you of little faith? With His own hands He has fastened your sins to the cross. But if, by chance, you fear to have recourse to Jesus because the majesty of God in Him overawes you — for though He became man he did not cease to be God — and you want another advocate with this divine mediator, go to Mary, for she will intercede for you with her Son, who will most certainly hear her. Then He will intercede with His Father who can deny nothing to such a Son."

And he concludes: "This loving Mother, O my children, is the ladder of sinners by which they re-ascend to the height of divine grace. She is our greatest confidence. She is the whole ground of my hope."

The words of the Canticle of Canticles can be applied to Mary; she is as "beautiful as the curtains of Solomon." (1:4) In the tents of David questions of war were treated; in those of Solomon questions of peace only were entertained. So, this Mother of mercy never treats of war and vengeance against sinners, but only of peace and forgiveness for them.

Mary was prefigured by the dove which returned to Noah in the ark with an olive branch in its beak (Gn 8:11), as a pledge of peace which God granted to mankind. St. Bonaventure uses it to address Mary:

"You are that most faithful dove; you are the sure mediatrix between God and the world, lost in a spiritual deluge.

"You, by presenting yourself before God, have obtained peace and salvation for a lost world. You are that heavenly dove which brought to a lost world the olive branch of mercy since you, in the first place, gave us Jesus Christ who is the source of mercy."

Again, the rainbow seen by St. John, which circled the throne of God, was a figure of Mary: "And there was a rainbow around the throne." (Rv 4:3) The rainbow around the throne is

Mary who softens the judgment and sentence of God against sinners, meaning that she is always before God's tribunal, mitigating the chastisements due to sinners.

St. Bernardine of Siena says that: "It was of this rainbow that God spoke when He promised Noah that He would place it in the clouds as a sign of peace, that looking on it He might remember the eternal peace which He has covenanted with mankind."

For many writers, Mary is compared to the moon. St. Bonaventure writes: "As the moon is between the heavens and the earth, so does Mary continually place herself between God and sinners in order to appease our Lord in their regard, and to enlighten them to return to Him."

O, how many obstinate sinners does not this magnet of hearts draw each day to God! For thus did she call herself one day, saying to St. Bridget: "As the magnet attracts iron, so do I attract hearts." Yes, even the most hardened — to reconcile them to God.

We must not suppose that such prodigies are extraordinary events; they are everyday occurrences. For my own part I could relate many cases of the kind that have occurred on our missions, where certain sinners with hearts harder than iron, continued so through all the sermons, but no sooner did they hear the one on the mercies of Mary, than they were filled with compunction and returned to God.

St. John Chrysostom says that: "Another purpose for which the Blessed Virgin Mary was made the Mother of God was that she might obtain salvation for many who, on account of their wicked lives, could not be saved according to the rigor of divine justice, but might be so with the help of her sweet mercy and powerful maternal intercession."

And St. Anselm concludes: "If then, Mary was made the Mother of God on account of sinners, how can I, however great my sins may be, despair of pardon?"

St. Justin Martyr, calls Mary an arbitrator who takes our case and presents it to her Son, indeed, pleads our case before Him. St. Andrew of Crete calls her "a pledge, a security for our reconciliation with God."

## PRAYER

*O my most sweet Lady, since your office is to act as a mediatrix between God and sinners, I will address you in the words of St. Thomas of Villanova: "Fulfill your office in my behalf, O tender advocate. Do your work."*

*Say that my cause is not too difficult to gain, for I know, and all agree, that every cause, no matter how desperate, if undertaken by you, is never, and never will be lost.*

*On seeing your immense mercy and the very great desire of your most loving heart to help even the most abandoned, I take great courage in begging for your intercession.*

*Be with me before the throne of God.    Amen.*

CHAPTER VII

# ILLOS TUOS MISERICORDES
# OCULOS AD NOS CONVERTE
*Turn, Then, Your Eyes of Mercy Towards Us*

## Mary Our Guardian

### MARY IS ALL EYES TO PITY AND HELPS US IN OUR NECESSITIES

St. Epiphanius called Mary "many-eyed," indicating her vigilance in assisting us poor creatures in this world. St. Andrew Avellino referred to her as the "Heavenly Commissioner," since she carries so many messages of mercy into the world.

St. Bridget heard our Lord tell His Mother: "Lady, ask whatever you will." And what does Mary ask? St. Bridget heard her reply: "I ask mercy for sinners." It is if she had said: "You have made me the Mother of mercy, the refuge of sinners, the advocate of the miserable; so what can I ask for other than mercy for all of them?" "I ask mercy for the miserable."

"And so, O Mary, you are so filled with mercy," exclaimed St. Bonaventure, "so attentive in relieving the wretched, that it seems that you have no other desire, no other anxiety." Of these miserable ones, and sinners are among the most miserable, St. Bede the Venerable adds: "Mary is always praying to her Son for them."

"Even while living in the world," says St. Jerome, "Mary was filled with tenderness and compassion for the pains of others." As we have seen, her actions at the wedding feast of Cana are typical of her care for others.

It has been said that "honors change our manners." This may be true of those who live in the world. When they reach high estate, they forget the companions of their trials. This is not true of Mary. St. Peter Damian addresses Mary along these lines:

"Perhaps, now that you have been raised to the high dignity of Queen of Heaven, you will forget us poor creatures? Far be such a thought! It does not become the great compassion that reigns in the heart of Mary, ever to forget such misery as ours."

On this subject, St. Bonaventure applies to the Blessed Virgin the words addressed to Ruth: "May the Lord bless you, my daughter, you have been even more loyal now than before." (Rt 3:10); meaning to say: "if the compassion of Mary was great towards the miserable when living in this world, it is much greater now that she reigns in heaven."

He then gives the reason for this: "This holy Mother shows, by the innumerable graces that she obtains for us now, her greater mercy, for now she is better acquainted with our miseries. As the splendor of the sun surpasses that of the moon, so does the compassion of Mary, now that she is in heaven, surpass the compassion she had for us when in the world."

St. Agnes also revealed this to St. Bridget: "Our Queen, now that she is united to her Son in heaven, cannot forget her innate goodness; therefore she shows her compassion to all, even to the most impious of sinners; so much so that as the celestial and terrestrial bodies are all illumined by the sun, so there is no one in the world, who, if he asks for it, does not, through the intercession of Mary, partake of the divine mercy."

St. Bernard says that: "Mary has been made all to all, and opens her fullness and her merciful heart to all. The slave may receive redemption, the sick health, those in affliction comfort, the sinner pardon, all for the glory of God."

It was revealed to St. Gertrude that when these words are addressed with devotion to the most Blessed Virgin: "Turn, then, O most gracious advocate, your eyes of mercy towards us," Mary can not do otherwise than yield to the demand of whoever thus invokes her.

St. Hildebert addresses her, saying: "You, O Lady, teach us to hope for far greater graces than we deserve, since you never cease to dispense favors far, far beyond our merits."

And where did Mary learn this generosity? From her Son. St. Bonaventure answers the question: "For as we have a most merciful Lord, so we have a most merciful Lady. Our Lord is plenteous in mercy to all who call upon Him, and our Lady follows His example."

One day, when St. Gertrude was addressing these words to our Lady: "Turn your eyes of mercy towards us," she saw the Blessed Virgin pointing to the eyes of her Son, whom she held in her arms, and then said: "These are the most compassionate eyes that I can turn for their salvation towards all who call upon me."

How, then, is it possible that anyone can perish who recommends himself to this good Mother, since her Son, as God, promised her that for her love He will show as much mercy as she pleases to all who recommend themselves to her?

This our Lord revealed to St. Gertrude, allowing her to hear Him make the promise to His Mother in the following words: "In my omnipotence, O revered Mother, I have granted you the reconciliation of all sinners who devoutly invoke the aid of your compassion, in whatever way it may please you."

Should the thought of our sins ever discourage us, let us address the Mother of Mercy in these words: "O Lady, do not set up my sins against me, for I oppose your compassion to them.

Let it never be said that my sins could contend in judgment against your mercy which is far more powerful to obtain my pardon than my sins are to obtain my condemnation."

## PRAYER

*O greatest and most sublime of all God's creatures, most dear Virgin, I salute you from this earth, I a miserable and unfortunate rebel against my God, who deserve chastisements, not favors; justice, not mercy.*

*We rejoice that you are so rich in mercy and therefore so able to help us poor sinners. The greater is our poverty, the more you exert yourself to help and protect us.*

*O my Mother, you wept bitter tears over the death of your Son, who died for me. I beg you, offer these tears to God on my behalf and obtain for me true sorrow for my sins. Obtain for me, O Mary, that from this day forward I will never add anything contrary to the wishes of yourself and your Son.*

*Obtain for me that I may be faithful to my God and love Him during the remainder of my life.    Amen.*

# CHAPTER VIII

# ET JESUM, BENEDICTUM FRUCTUM VENTRIS TUI NOBIS POST HOC EXILIUM OSTENDE

*And after this, Our Exile, show unto Us the Blessed Fruit of Your Womb, Jesus*

## Mary, our Salvation

### i

### MARY DELIVERS HER CLIENTS FROM HELL

It is impossible for a client of Mary, who is faithful in honoring and recommending himself to her, to be lost. To some, this proposition may appear, at first sight, exaggerated. But anyone to whom this might seem to be the case I would beg to suspend judgment, and, first of all, read what I have to say on this subject.

When we say that it is impossible for a client of Mary to be lost, we must not be understood of speaking of those clients who take advantage of this devotion, that they may sin more freely. Those who disapprove of the great praises bestowed on the mercy of Mary, because it causes the wicked to take advantage of it to sin with greater freedom, do so without foundation, for such presumptive people deserve chastisement, and not mercy for their rash presumption.

It is therefore to be understood of those clients who, with a sincere desire to amend their lives, are faithful in honoring and recommending themselves to the Mother of God. It is, I say, morally impossible that such as these should be lost.

Contemporary theologians say the same thing, but that we may see that they did not speak at random; let us examine what the saints have said on this subject. Do not be surprised if many of these quotations are alike, since I want to show how unanimous they are on this subject.

St. Anselm says that: "As it is impossible for one who is not devout to Mary, and consequently not protected by her, to be saved, so it is impossible for one who recommends himself to her, and consequently is beloved by her, to be lost."

St. Antoninus repeats the same thing in almost the same words: "As it is impossible for those from whom Mary turns her eyes of mercy to be saved, so also are those towards whom she turns those eyes, and for whom she prays, necessarily saved and glorified."

Let us pay particular attention to the first part of these opinions of these saints, and let those tremble who make but little account of their devotion to this Blessed Mother, or who from carelessness give it up. They claim that the salvation of those not protected by Mary is impossible.

Many others say the same thing. St. Albert the Great says that: "All who are not the servants of Mary will perish." And St. Bonaventure: "He who neglects the service of the blessed Virgin will die in his sins." Again: "He who does not invoke you, O Lady, will never get to heaven."

Before him, St. Ignatius, the martyr, had said that: "It was impossible for any sinner to be saved without the help and favor of the most Blessed Virgin; because those who are not saved by the justice of God are, with great mercy, saved by the intercession of Mary." St. John Chrysostom adopted these same words.

St. Hilary observed that: "However great a sinner may have been, if he shows himself devout to Mary, he will never perish." For this reason the devil does his utmost with sinners, in order that, after they have lost the grace of God, they may also lose devotion to Mary.

St. Ephrem was right then, in calling devotion to our Blessed Lady "a charter of liberty," our safeguard from hell. The same saint also calls the blessed Mother "the only hope of those who are in despair."

That which St. Bernard says is certainly true, that "neither the power nor the will to save us can be wanting in Mary"; the power cannot be wanting, for it is impossible that her prayers should not be heard. St. Antoninus declares: "It is impossible that the Mother of God should pray in vain." St. Bernard repeats: "Her requests can never be refused, but she obtains whatever she wills."

Since then this is the case, how can it be possible for a client of Mary to be lost? He may be a sinner, but if he recommends himself to this good Mother with perseverance and the firm purpose of amendment, she will undertake to obtain for him light to abandon his wicked state, sorrow for his sins, perseverance in virtue and, finally, a good death.

What mother would not deliver her son from death if it only depended on her asking the favor to obtain it from the judge? Can we think that Mary, who loves her clients with a mother's most tender love, will not deliver her child from eternal death when she can do it so easily?

Ah, devout reader, let us thank our Lord if we see that He has given us affection for the Queen of Heaven, and confidence in her, for, says St. John Chrysostom: "God only grants this favor to those whom He is determined to save."

Therefore Erasmus salutes the Blessed Virgin in these words: "Hail! O terror of hell; O, hope of Christians; confidence in you is a pledge of salvation."

How enraged is the devil when he sees a soul persevering in devotion to the Blessed Mother! We read in the life of St. Alphonsus Rodriguez, who was a devout client of Mary, that once, when in prayer, he was much troubled by the devil. This enemy said to him: "Give up your devotion to Mary and I will cease to torment you."

Blosius tells us that God revealed to St. Catherine of Siena that: "In His goodness and on account of the Incarnate Word, He had granted to Mary, who was His Mother, that no one, not even a sinner, who devoutly recommends himself to her should ever become the prey of hell."

"O how many would have remained obstinate in sin, and would have been eternally lost," says Thomas a Kempis, "if Mary had not interposed with her Son, that He might show them mercy."

Blessed Henry Suso used to say that: "He had placed his soul in the hands of Mary, and that if he was condemned, the sentence must pass through her hands."

Pray, then, for us, O holy Mother of God, that we may be preserved from hell. Defend me, O Mother of mercy, that the Judge may be favorable to me at the hour of death. With great confidence, I hope to praise you and love you forever.

# PRAYER

*O Mary, my most dear Mother, in what an abyss of evils should I not now be if you had not so many times delivered me by your powerful intercession. How many years ago should I not have been in hell if you had not saved me by your powerful prayers.*

*You overcame the hardness of my heart and drew me to your love and to confidence in you. Your compassionate hands has led me through countless dangers and helped me when I was on the point of falling.*

*Continue, O my hope, to preserve me from hell and from the temptations that will still beset my paths in the time to come. Obtain for me the great treasure of remaining faithful to my God and to you, my patroness.*

*I hope to love you always, in time and in eternity. Amen.*

## ii

### MARY HELPS HER CLIENTS IN PURGATORY

Fortunate, indeed, are the clients of this most compassionate Mother. Not only does she help them in this world but even in purgatory they have her help and protection.

And as in that prison the poor souls are in the greatest need of assistance, since in their torments they cannot help themselves, our Mother of mercy does proportionately more to relieve them. St. Bernardine of Siena says that: "In that prison, where souls that are spouses of Jesus Christ are detained, Mary has a certain dominion and plenitude of power, not only to relieve them, but even to deliver them from their pains."

The blessed Mother once addressed these words to St. Bridget: "I am the Mother of all the souls in purgatory; for all the pains they have deserved for their sins are, every hour, as long as they are detained there, in some way mitigated by my prayers."

"O, how courteous and loving is the most Blessed Virgin,"

says St. Vincent Ferrer, "to those who suffer in purgatory! Through her they constantly receive comfort and refreshment."

Mary not only consoles and relieves her clients in purgatory, but she delivers them by her prayers. St. Bernardine of Siena was of the opinion that: "The Blessed Virgin has the power of delivering souls from purgatory, but particularly those of her clients, by her prayers and by applying her own merits for them." She has only to ask and all is done.

Just as a great king might grant amnesty and free the prisoners on the occasion of some great festivity, it was the opinion of many saints and writers that Christ the King does the same for those imprisoned in purgatory. And if this is true of such feasts as Easter, Pentecost and Christmas, the Queen of Heaven could be expected to do the same on her great festal days.

The feast of the Assumption was a favorite among saints such as St. Peter Damian, St. Bernard, St. Bernardine of Siena and writers such as Gerson, Novarinus and Denis the Carthusian. The latter pictures Mary as going there with a company of angels and saints to help them celebrate her festivities. There she would free great numbers, "more than all the population of Rome."

The promise made by our Blessed Lady to Pope John XXII is well known. She appeared to him and ordered him to make known to all that in the Saturday after their death she would deliver from purgatory all who wore the Carmelite scapular. This was proclaimed by that pontiff in a Bull, and it was confirmed in subsequent years by Alexander V, Pius V, Gregory XIII and Paul V.

In a Bull dated 1613, Pope Paul V says that: "Christian people may piously believe that the Blessed Virgin will help them after death by her continual intercession, her merits, and special protection; and that on Saturday, the day set aside by the Church for devotion to her, she will in a more particular manner help the souls of the members of the Confraternity of our Blessed Lady of Mount Carmel who have departed this life in a state of grace, provided they have worn the habit (scapular), observed the chastity of their state in life, and recited her office: or if they could not recite it, if they have observed the fasts of the Church, and abstained from meat on all Wednesdays, except Christmas-day."

In the solemn office of our Blessed Lady of Mount Carmel, we read that it is piously believed that the Blessed Virgin comforts the members of this confraternity in purgatory with maternal love, and that by her intercession she soon delivers them and takes them to heaven.

We can hope for the same graces and favors if we are devout clients of this good Mother. And, if we serve her with more special love, we can hope to go to heaven immediately after death, without even going to purgatory.

This really took place in the case of Blessed Godfrey (Geoffrey). The Blessed Mother sent him this message through one of the brothers: "Tell Brother Godfrey to endeavor to advance rapidly in virtue, and thus he will belong to my Son and to me: and when his soul departs, I will not allow him to go to purgatory, but will take his soul and offer it to my Son."

Finally, if we wish to relieve the holy souls in purgatory, let us do so by imploring the aid of our Blessed Lady in all our prayers, and especially by offering the Rosary for them, as that relieves them greatly.

## PRAYER

*O Queen of heaven and earth! O Mother of the Lord of the World! O Mary, of all creatures the greatest, the most exalted, the most amiable! It is true that there are many in this world who neither know you nor love you, but in heaven*

*there are many millions of angels and blessed spirits who love
you and praise you continually.*

*Even in this world, how many happy souls there are who burn
with love for you, and live enamored of your goodness! How
many there are who continually thank God for all that He has
effected in your soul!*

*O my most dear Mother, help me to love you as I should. Help
me to do all that I can to bring others to love you with sincere
hearts. Then, assist me at the time of my death, deliver me
from purgatory and lead me to your Son in heaven.    Amen.*


## iii

### MARY LEADS HER SERVANTS TO HEAVEN

O, what an evident mark of predestination have the servants of
Mary! Blessed is he whose soul offers the Blessed Virgin a place
of repose. Devotion towards the Blessed Mother remains in all
who are the inheritance of the Lord, that is to say, in all who will
praise Him for all eternity. Blessed indeed is the person who
grows in devotion to Mary and perseveres in it.

Applying the words of Ecclesiasticus, the Church has Mary
say: "He that made me rested in my tabernacle, and He said to
me: Let your dwelling be in Jacob and your inheritance in Israel,
and take root in my chosen one." (24:8 ff.)

That is, my Creator had condescended to come and repose
with me and His will is that I should dwell in the hearts of all the
elect (of whom Jacob was a figure, and who are the inheritance of
the Blessed Virgin), and that devotion and confidence in me
should take root in all the predestined.

O, how many blessed souls are now in heaven who would
never have been there had not Mary, by her powerful inter-

cession, led them there. St. Bonaventure says that: "The gates of heaven will open to all who confide in the protection of Mary."

Therefore, St. Ephrem calls devotion to the Blessed Mother "the unlocking of the gates of the heavenly Jerusalem." We can pray with St. Ambrose: "Open to us, O Mary, the gates of paradise, since you have its keys." Indeed, in the Litany of Loretto, holy Church addresses Mary as "Gate of Heaven. . . ."

Holy Church also frequently addresses Mary as the "Star of the Sea." St. Thomas Aquinas says: "As sailors are guided by a star to the port, so are Christians guided to heaven by Mary." St. Bernard cries out: "Look up to the star. Call upon Mary."

St. Fulgentius calls Mary, "the heavenly ladder." "For," the saint adds, "by Mary God descended into the world, that by her men might ascend from earth to heaven." Or as St. Athanasius puts it: "You, O Lady, were filled with grace that you might be the way of our salvation and the means of ascent to the heavenly kingdom."

"Blessed are they who know you, O Mother of God," writes St. Bonaventure, "for knowledge of you is the high road to everlasting life, and the publication of your virtues is the way to eternal salvation."

Denis the Carthusian asks: "Who is there that is saved? Who is there that reigns in heaven?" And he answers: "They are certainly saved and reign in heaven for whom this Queen of mercy interceded."

And applying this verse from Proverbs to Mary, "By me kings reign" (8:15), she says that through her intercession, souls reign, first in this mortal life by ruling their passions, and so come to reign eternally in heaven where, notes St. Augustine, "all are kings."

Our Blessed Lady, being Mother of the Lord of Heaven, it is reasonable that she should also be sovereign Lady of that kingdom where by right she rules with her Son over all, forever.

St. Antoninus tells us that: "This blessed Mother has

already, by her assistance and prayers, obtained heaven for us, provided we put no obstacle in the way." St. John Damascene adds: "To serve Mary and be her courtier is the greatest honor we can possible possess; for to serve the Queen of heaven is already to reign there, and to live under her command is more than to govern."

"May the infinite goodness of our Lord be ever praised," says St. Bernard, "for having been pleased to give us Mary as our advocate in heaven, that she, being at the same time the Mother of the Judge and a Mother of mercy, may be able, by her intercession, to conduct to a prosperous issue the great affair of our eternal salvation."

St. James the Monk, a Doctor of the Greek Church, says that: "God destined Mary as a bridge of salvation, by using which we might with safety pass over the stormy sea of this world, and reach the happy haven of paradise."

St. Bonaventure exclaims: "Give ear, O nations, and all who desire heaven; serve, honor Mary and certainly you will find eternal life." St. Germanus adds: "O, how many sinners have found God and have been saved by means of Mary!"

We read in the life of the servant of God, Sister Seraphina of Capri, that once, during the novena for the feast of the Assumption of Mary, she asked Mary for the conversion of a thousand sinners. Afterwards, she was afraid that she had asked too much. Instead, our Lady appeared to her and asked: "Is it that you fear I am not powerful enough to grant such a request? See, the favor has already been granted." And she showed her the multitude of sinners she had saved by her intercession.

St. Bernard writes that devotion to the Mother of God is a most certain mark of eternal salvation. Blessed Alan, speaking of the 'Hail Mary,' also says that: "Whoever often honors our Blessed Lady with this angelic salutation has a very great mark of predestination." He repeats this same thing about perseverance in the daily recital of the Rosary.

St. Mary Magdalen de Pazzi saw a vessel in the midst of the sea; in it were all the clients of Mary, and this Blessed Mother herself steered it safely into the port. By this the saint understood that those who live under her protection are secure, in the midst of the dangers of this life, from the shipwreck of sin and from eternal damnation. Mary guides them safely into the haven of salvation.

Let us then enter this blessed ship of the mantle of Mary, and there we can be certain of the kingdom of heaven. For holy Church says: "O holy Mother of God, all those who want to be partakers of eternal happiness dwell with you, living under your protection."

## PRAYER

*O Queen of Heaven, Mother of holy love! Since you are the most amiable of creatures, the most beloved of God, and His greatest lover, help us who are living in this world to love you and serve you.*

*I would like to spread the knowledge of your power and love among all the peoples on this earth. I would like to praise your dignity as Mother of God, the glory of your perpetual virginity and the privilege of your Immaculate Conception before the whole world.*

*Ah! my most beloved Mother, accept my ardent desire and never allow me, your servant, to become an enemy of God who loves you so much. I am not discouraged because of my past sins, because I know how much you love even the most wretched of sinners.*

*Pray to Jesus for me. Nothing else is needed. Let me always sing the praises of Mary.    Amen.*

# CHAPTER IX

# O CLEMENS, O PIA!

### CLEMENCY AND COMPASSION OF MARY:
### HOW GREAT ARE THE CLEMENCY
### AND COMPASSION OF MARY

St. Bernard, speaking of the great compassion of Mary towards us poor creatures, says that: "She is the land overflowing with milk and honey promised by God." And St. Leo observes that: "The Blessed Virgin has so merciful a heart that she deserves not only to be called merciful, but mercy itself."

As St. Bonaventure addresses her: "O Lady, when I behold you, I can only see mercy! For you were made the Mother of God for the wretched, and then you were entrusted with their charge. You are totally solicitous for them, so replete with mercy that you wish only the opportunity to dispense it."

"And what," exclaims St. Bernard, "can ever flow from a source of compassion but compassion itself."

Mary is also likened to an olive tree: "As a fair olive tree on the plains." (Ec 24:19) For, as from the olive tree, oil, a symbol of mercy, alone is extracted, so from the hands of Mary favors and mercy alone proceed. When we go to her for the oil of her mercy, we cannot fear that she will deny it to us, as the wise virgins did to the foolish, for fear there would not be enough. No, for Mary is rich indeed in this oil of mercy.

Mary is called by the Church not simply a prudent Virgin, but "Virgin most prudent." She is so full of grace and compassion that she can supply all, without losing any herself.

Note that this oil tree is pictured as standing on a plain, not surrounded by a garden or a wall. This is so that she may stand out and be approached by all who need the gift of mercy. As St. Antoninus explains it, it is so because: "All can go to, and gather the fruit of this olive tree, exposed on all sides, and both the just and the sinner can have recourse to her."

He adds: "O how many sentences of condemnation has not this most Blessed Virgin revoked by her compassionate prayers, in favor of sinners who had recourse to her."

Thomas a Kempis concurs: "What safer refuge can we ever find than the compassionate heart of Mary? There the poor find a home, the infirm a remedy, the afflicted relief, the doubtful counsel, and the abandoned succor."

Wretched, indeed, should we be, had we not this Mother of mercy always attentive and solicitous to relieve us in our wants. "Where there is no woman, he mourns that he is in want." (Ec 36:27) "This woman," says St. John Damascene, "is precisely the most Blessed Virgin Mary; and wherever this woman is not, the sick man groans."

And surely it cannot be otherwise, since all graces are dispensed at the prayer of Mary. Where this is wanting, there can be no hope of mercy, as our Lord gave St. Bridget to understand in these words: "Unless the prayers of Mary interposed, there could be no hope of mercy."

But perhaps we hear that Mary does not see, does not feel for, our necessities? O no, she sees and feels for them far better than we do ourselves. "There is not one among all the saints," says St. Antoninus, "who can ever feel for us in our miseries, both corporal and spiritual, like this woman, the most Blessed Mother Mary." So much so that when she see misery, she cannot do otherwise than instantly fly to relieve it with her tender compassion.

Suetonius relates that the Emperor Titus was so desirous of rendering service to those who applied to him, that, when a day passed without being able to grant a favor, he used to say with sorrow: "I have lost a day, for I have spent it without benefiting any one." It is probable that Titus spoke more from vanity and the desire to be esteemed, than from true charity.

But such a thing could not happen with our Empress Mary, so great is her charity. She is more anxious to grant us favors than we are to receive them. Whenever we go to her, we always find her hands filled with mercy and liberality.

Rebecca was a figure of Mary, and she, when asked by Abraham's servant for a little water to drink, replied that she would give him plenty of water for himself and for his animals, as well. "I will draw water for your camels, too, until they all have their fill of water." (Gn 24:19)

On these words St. Bernard addresses our Blessed Lady, saying: "O Mary, you are far more liberal and compassionate than Rebecca. Therefore you are not satisfied with distributing the treasure of your immense mercy only to the just, of whom Abraham's servants were types, but you also give them to sinners, who are signified by the camels."

The liberality of Mary is like that of her Son, who always gives more than He is asked for. "He is rich to all who call upon Him." (Rm 10:12) Since the liberality of Mary's is like His, she, too, bestows more than is sought.

Hear the prayer of a devotee as he addressed the Blessed Virgin: "Pray for me, O Lady, for you will ask for the graces I require with greater devotion than I can dare to ask for them; and you will obtain far greater graces for me from God than I can presume to seek."

When the Samaritans refused to receive Jesus Christ and His doctrines, St. James and St. John asked Him whether they should command fire to fall from heaven and devour them. Our Lord rebuked them, since He was not of this spirit to avenge himself. (Lk 9:55)

It is as if He had said to them: "I am of so tender and compassionate a spirit that I came from heaven to save and not to chastise sinners, and you wish to see them lost. Fire, indeed! Punishment, indeed! Speak no more of such chastisements for such a spirit is not mine."

And so with Mary, whose spirit is the same as that of her Son, we can never doubt that she is all-inclined to mercy. As she said to St. Bridget, she is called the Mother of mercy, and it was by God's own mercy that she was made so compassionate and sweet towards all.

We frequently apply the words of the Book of Revelation to our Lady: "And a great sign appeared in the heavens, a woman clothed with the sun." (12:1) On these words, St. Bernard, turning towards the Blessed Virgin says: "You, O Lady have clothed the sun, that is the Eternal Word, with human flesh. He has clothed you with His power and His mercy."

"This Queen," he continues, "is so compassionate and loving, that when a sinner, whoever he may be, recommends himself to her charity, she does not question his merits, or whether he is worthy or unworthy to be heeded, but she hears and helps everyone."

"And therefore," remarks St. Idelbert, "Mary is said to be 'fair as the moon. (Cant 6:9) For as the moon enlightens and benefits the lowest creatures on earth, so does Mary enlighten and help the most unworthy sinners." The moon receives all its light from the sun, as Mary receives all her power from the Son.

Our sins may cause us to fear to approach the Almighty,

because it is His infinite majesty that we have offended. We must never fear to go to Mary, for in her we shall find nothing to terrify us. True, she is holy, immaculate, and the Queen of the world, but she is also of our flesh, and like us, a child of Adam.

"How long since," exclaims St. Fulgentius, "would the world have been destroyed, had not Mary sustained it by her powerful intercession!"

In commenting on these word: "O clement, O loving, O sweet Virgin Mary," St. Bonaventure was led to pray: "O Mary, you are clement with the miserable, compassionate towards those who pray to you, and sweet towards those who love you; clement with the penitent, compassionate towards those who advance in virtue, and sweet to the perfect. You show yourself clement in delivering us from punishment, loving in bestowing favors, and sweet in giving yourself to all who seek you."

## PRAYER

*Mother of mercy, you are so compasssionate and so willing to help us, I come before you with this request. Obtain for me from our Lord all that you know I need to be pleasing to Him.*

*Others may rightly seek bodily health, earthly goods, power or position. I want only what is conformable to your loving and compassionate heart.*

*You are completely filled with the love of God; obtain for me the gift of His holy love. You are so humble, help me grow in true humility. You were so patient under suffering in this life, help me be patient in trials. You are entirely conformed to the divine will, help me seek the will of God with the courage to follow wherever it leads.*

*With your help, encourage me in the service of your Son, our God. Amen.*

# CHAPTER X

# O DULCIS VIRGO MARIA
## *O Sweet Virgin Mary*

### THE SWEETNESS OF THE NAME OF MARY DURING LIFE AND AT DEATH

The great name of Mary, which was given to the Blessed Mother, did not come to her from her parents alone, nor was it given to her simply by the mind or will of man, as is the case other names given in this world. This name came from heaven and was given by a divine ordinance. This is attested to by St. Jerome, St. Epiphanius, St. Antoninus and many others.

"The name of Mary came from the treasury of the divinity," says St. Peter Damian. And the holy anchorite Honorius used to say that: "This name of Mary is filled with every sweetness and divine blessing."

"The name of Jesus," noted St. Bernard, "is joy in the heart, honey in the mouth and melody to the ear." St. Anthony of Padua borrowed this to tell of the sweetness that Mary's clients find in her name, too.

Blessed Juvenal Ancina used to taste the joy of Mary's name on his lips, physically, so great and sensible a sweetness was it. But here I intend to speak of the salutary sweetness of consolation, of love, of joy, of confidence, of strength, which the name of Mary ordinarily brings to those who pronounce it with devotion.

After the most sacred name of Jesus, the name of Mary is rich in every good thing on earth and in heaven. There is something so admirable, sweet and blessed in this name of Mary that when it meets with friendly hearts it breathes into them a delightful sweetness. If heard a thousand times, it is always heard with a renewed pleasure.

Blessed Henry Suso said that: "When he named Mary he felt himself so excited to confidence, so inflamed with love and joy, that he was overcome with tears and joy. O Mary, what must you be like if your very name alone is so amiable and gracious!"

The enamored St. Bernard, raising his heart to his good Mother exclaims with confidence: "O great! O pious! so worthy of all praise! O most holy Virgin Mary! Your name is so sweet and amiable that it cannot be pronounced without inflaming those who do so with love towards you and God. It need only occur in thoughts to those who love you to move them to love you more and to console them."

As St. Methodius concludes: "Your name, O Mother of God, is filled with heavenly graces and blessings." St. Bonaventure declares: "Your name, O Mary, cannot be pronounced without bringing some blessing to those who do so devoutly."

Blessed Raymond Jordan says that: "However hardened and difficult a heart may be, the name of this most Blessed Virgin has such efficacy that if it is only pronounced that heart will be wonderfully softened." And he concludes: "Through you the sinner recovers the hope of forgiveness and grace."

For this reason, the holy name of Mary is likened in the sacred canticles to oil: "Your name is as oil poured out." (Office B.V.M.) St. Ambrose states that her name: "Is a precious ointment which breathes forth the odor of divine grace." Blessed Alan says that the glory of her name is compared to oil poured out because oil heals the sick, sends out a sweet odor, and nourishes flames.

The devils flee at the mention of her name, as is testified to by Thomas a Kempis: "That hearing the name of Queen of Heaven they fly from the one pronouncing her name as man flies from a burning fire." The Blessed Virgin herself confirmed this to St. Bridget.

St. Germanus declares that: "As breathing is a sign of life, so also is the frequent pronouncement of the name of Mary a sign either of the life of divine grace, or that it will soon come; for this powerful name has in it the virtue of obtaining life and help for the one who invoked it devoutly."

Let us always take advantage of the beautiful advice given us by St. Bernard in these words: "In danger, in perplexities, in doubtful cases, think of Mary, call on Mary. Let her name not leave your lips; let her not depart from your heart."

In every danger of losing divine grace we should think of Jesus and Mary and invoke their names together; for these two names always go together. Never let us permit that these two most sweet names leave our lips or our hearts. They will give us the strength to conquer all of our temptations.

Consoling, indeed, are the promises of help made by Jesus Christ to those who have devotion to the name of Mary. One day, in the hearing of St. Bridget, He promised His most holy Mother that He would grant three special graces to those who invoke her holy name with confidence: first, that He would grant them perfect sorrow for their sins; second, that their crimes should be atoned for; and third, that He would give them the strength to attain perfection and at length, the glory of paradise.

And then our Divine Savior added: "For your words, O my

Mother, are so sweet and agreeable to me, that I cannot deny what you ask."

St. Ephrem goes so far as to say that: "The name of Mary is the key to the gates of heaven," in the hands of those who devoutly invoke it.

Thomas a Kempis draws this conclusion: "If you desire consolation in every labor, have recourse to Mary; invoke the name of Mary, honor Mary, recommend yourselves to Mary; rejoice with Mary; weep with Mary; walk with Mary; seek Jesus with Mary; desire to live and die with Jesus and Mary. By acting thus you will always advance in the ways of God, for Mary will most willingly pray for you, and the Son will most certainly grant all that His Mother asks."

And so we see that the most holy name of Mary is sweet indeed to her clients during life on account of the very great graces she obtains for them. But sweeter still will it be to them in death on account of the tranquil and holy end that it will insure for them.

This name of life and hope, when repeated at the hour of death, suffices to put devils to flight and to comfort the dying in their sufferings. "The invocation of the sacred name of Jesus and Mary," offers Thomas a Kempis, "is a short prayer which is as sweet to the mind, and as powerful to protect those who use it against the enemies of their salvation, as it is easy to remember."

St. Camillus de Lellis urged the members of his community to remind the dying often to utter the holy names of Jesus and Mary. Such was his custom when assisting people in their last hour. When he himself died, he gave an edifying example of his confidence in the holy names. His last words were the sacred names of Jesus and Mary.

Let us, then, devout reader, beg God to grant us, at the moment of death, that the last word on our lips may be the name of Mary.

## PRAYER

*O great Mother of God and my Mother Mary, it is true that I am unworthy to pronounce your name. Yet you love me and you desire my salvation. May I always invoke your most holy and powerful name during life and at the point of death.*

*During times of joy and sorrow, let me repeat your name, Mary, Mary. In times of trial and temptation, let me invoke your name, Mary, Mary. When I need help and strength, let me call on you, Mary, Mary.*

*I thank my Lord and God for giving me the knowledge of your name, so powerful in time of need. And let my last words be, "I love you, O Jesus; I love you, O Mary; to you do I give my heart and my soul." Amen.*

# PART TWO
## DISCOURSES ON THE PRINCIPAL FEASTS
## OF MARY

DISCOURSES

---

# DISCOURSES ON THE PRINCIPAL FEASTS OF MARY

---

## I.

## MARY'S IMMACULATE CONCEPTION
### *December 8*

HOW FITTING IT WAS THAT EACH OF THE
THREE DIVINE PERSONS SHOULD PRESERVE MARY
FROM ORIGINAL SIN.

Great indeed was the injury that fell on Adam and all his posterity by his accursed sin. He not only lost sanctifying grace for himself, but he also lost all the other precious gifts with which he had originally been endowed. Furthermore he lost all these for his descendants and earned for the race an enmity with God.

God was pleased to exempt the Blessed Virgin from this tragedy because He had destined her to be the Mother of the Second Adam, Jesus Christ, who was to repair the evil done by the first. Now let us see how fitting it was that God, all the three divine Persons, should preserve her; that the Father should preserve her as His Daughter, the Son as His Mother and the Holy Spirit as His Spouse.


*i*


In the first place it was fitting that the Eternal Father should preserve Mary from the stain of original sin, because she was His daughter, and His first-born daughter if we apply the words of Scripture to her: "I came forth from the mouth of the Most High, the first-born of all creatures." (Ec24:5) Many interpreters of holy Scripture, many Fathers of the Church, and holy Church itself apply these words to her.

Some call her the first-born because of the eternal decree that predestined her with her Son, before all creatures. Some call her the first-born of grace as the predestined Mother of the Redeemer. All agree in calling her the first-born of God.

It was quite becoming that Mary should never have been the slave of Lucifer, but only and always possessed by her Creator. "The Lord possessed me in the beginning of His ways." (Prov 8:22) Denis of Alexandria calls her "the one and only daughter of life," in contradistinction to others who, being born in sin, are daughters of death.

Besides this, it was quite becoming that the Eternal Father should create her in His grace, since He destined her to be the repairer of the lost world, the mediatrix of peace between God and man. As such she is observed and described by many of the holy Fathers.

Thus St. John Damascene addresses her: "O Blessed Virgin, you were born to minister to the salvation of the whole world." St. Bernard says that: "Noah's ark was a type of Mary, for as by means of it men were preserved from the deluge, so are we all saved from the shipwreck of sin: but with this difference, that in the ark few were saved, and through Mary the whole human race was rescued from death."

St. Athanasius called her "the new Eve, and the Mother of Life"; and not without reason, for the first was the Mother of death, but the most Blessed Virgin was the Mother of true Life. St. Theophanius of Nice adds: "Hail, you who have taken away Eve's sorrow!"

It certainly would not be becoming to choose an enemy to treat of peace with the offended person, and still less an accomplice in the crime itself. Since Mary was to be the mediatrix of peace between God and men, it was of the utmost importance that she should not herself appear as a sinner and as an enemy of God, but that she should appear in all things as a friend, and free from every stain of sin.

Still more was it becoming that God should preserve her from original sin, for He destined her to crush the head of that infernal spirit, which by seducing our first parents, entailed death upon all men. "I will put enmities between you and the woman, between your seed and her seed: he shall crush your head." (Gn 3:15)

Above all, it principally became the Eternal Father to preserve this, His daughter, unspotted by Adam's sin, because He destined her to be the Mother of His Son. If then, for no other reason, at least for the honor of His Son, who was God, it was reasonable that the Father should create Mary free from every stain of sin.

St. Thomas Aquinas teaches that "holiness is attributed to those things that are ordained for God." Certainly the Father who destined Mary to be the Mother of His own Son would adorn her soul with all the most precious gifts, that she might be a dwelling worthy of God!

*ii*

In the second place, it was becoming that the Son should preserve Mary from sin, as being His Mother. No man can choose his own mother, but if such a thing were ever granted, would he not choose a most noble lady?

If, then the Son of God alone could choose a Mother according to His own heart, His own liking, we must consider, as a matter of fact, that He would choose one becoming to God. And as it was becoming that a most pure God should have a Mother pure from all sin, He created her spotless.

St. Bernardine of Siena speaks of the eminence of sanctifications that God bestowed upon her, "which certainly included the entire removal of original sin."

St. Ambrose calls Mary, "a heavenly vessel," not because Mary was not earthly by nature, but because she was heavenly by grace. She was as far superior to the angels of heaven in sanctity and purity, as it was becoming that she should be, in whose womb the King of glory was to dwell.

To St. Bridget these words were revealed: "Mary was conceived without sin, that the divine Son might be born of her without sin." Mary was not only the Mother, but the worthy Mother of our Savior.

Since God created Mary worthy to be the Mother of His Son, "what excellency and what perfection was there that did not become her?" asks St. Thomas of Villanova. St. Thomas Aquinas responds: "When God chooses anyone for a particular dignity, He renders him fit for it"; and he adds that: "God, having chosen Mary for His Mother, He also by His grace rendered her worthy of this highest of all dignities."

St. Augustine tells us that when speaking of Mary he would not entertain even the question of sin in her. And he says further: "The Son of God never made Himself a more worthy dwelling than Mary, who was never possessed by the enemy or despoiled of her ornaments."

St. Methodius reminds us that: "He who said 'Honor your father and your mother', that He might observe His own decree gave all grace and honor to His own Mother." But how little Jesus would have guarded His Mother's honor had He not preserved her from Adam's sin! Jesus came as a liberator for all the rest of mankind; to the most Blessed Virgin He was a pre-liberator.

All the others had a Redeemer who delivered them from sin with which they were already defiled. The most Blessed Virgin had a Redeemer, who, because He was her Son, preserved her from ever being defiled by it.

## iii

Since, then, it was becoming that the Father should preserve Mary from sin as His Daughter, and the Son as His Mother, it was also becoming that the Holy Spirit should preserve her as His Spouse.

St. Augustine says that: "Mary was that only one who merited to be called the Mother and the Spouse of God." For St. Anselm asserts that: "The Holy Spirit, the love itself of the Father and the Son, came corporally into Mary, and enriching her with grace above all creatures, reposed in her and made her His Spouse, the Queen of heaven and earth."

He says "corporally," that is, as to the effect: for He came to form of her immaculate body the immaculate body of Jesus Christ, as the Archangel had already predicted to her: "The Holy Spirit will come upon you." (Lk 1:35) The flesh of Jesus, both before and after the Resurrection, was the flesh of Mary.

And it is, therefore, as St. Thomas teaches that: "Mary is called the temple of the Lord, and the sacred resting place of the Holy Spirit: for by the operation of the Holy Spirit she became the Mother of the Incarnate Word."

Now, had an excellent artist the power to make his bride such as he could represent her, what pains would he not take to render her as beautiful as possible! Who, then, can say that the Holy Spirit did otherwise with Mary, when He could make her who was to be His Spouse as beautiful as it became Him that she should be?

He acted as it became Him to act, as we apply the inspired words to Mary: "You are all beautiful, O my love, and there is not a spot in you." (Cant 4:7) These words, according to many saints and scholars, are properly to be understood of Mary. Indeed, St. Bernardine of Siena and St. Lawrence Justinian understood them precisely as applying to the Immaculate Conception.

This is why the Archangel Gabriel found her, before she became the Mother of God, full of grace and saluted her that way: "Hail, full of grace!" St. Sophronius notes that: "Grace is given partially to other saints, but to the Blessed Virgin all was given."

From the moment of Mary's conception she was enriched and filled with grace; the plenitude of grace was in her by the outpouring of the Holy Spirit.

## * Editorial Note

St. Alphonsus concludes with a very lengthy section discussing the reasons for this devotion to Mary Immaculate. He quotes an impressive number of saints and theologians who taught about the Immaculate Conception. He even states his own conviction that this was a doctrine that could some day be defined.

One hundred years later Pope Pius IX, on December 8, 1854, proclaimed, solemnly, the doctrine of Mary's Immaculate Conception:

"We define the doctrine which holds that the most blessed Virgin Mary was, from the first instant of her conception, by a singular privilege by the omnipotent grace of God, through the application of the merits of Jesus Christ, the Savior of the human race, preserved immune from all the fault of original sin, that this is revealed by God and is to be believed by all the faithful, firmly and constantly."

It was the Franciscan, John Duns Scotus (died 1308) who first suggested that Mary was kept free of original sin by a "preservative redemption" — in anticipation of the foreseen merits of Jesus Christ — the explanation eventually recognized as revealed truth.

---

# II
# THE BIRTH OF MARY
## *September 8*

MARY WAS BORN A SAINT AND A GREAT SAINT; FOR
THE GRACE WITH WHICH GOD ENRICHED HER FROM
THE BEGINNING WAS GREAT, AND THE FIDELITY
WITH WHICH SHE IMMEDIATELY CORRESPONDED TO
IT WAS GREAT

Men usually rejoice at the birth of a child, and it is a cause for great joy. It is also a time of sorrow, since the child is born into a world of sin, lacking in the friendship of God.

It is right, however, to rejoice in the birth of Mary with festivity and universal joy. She first saw the light of day a babe, in point of age, but great in merit and virtue. Mary was born a saint, and a great saint.

To form an idea of the greatness of her sanctity we must examine two things: the greatness of the first grace with which God enriched her, and then the greatness of her fidelity in immediately corresponding to it.

*i*

It is certain that Mary's soul was the most beautiful that God ever created; nay, more, after the work of the Incarnation of the Eternal Word, this was the greatest and most worthy of Himself that an omnipotent God ever did in the world.

The opinion of the theologians is general and certain, that the grace received by the Blessed Virgin exceeded not only that of any particular saint, but of all the angels and saints put together. It is also their teaching that Mary received this grace in the first instance of her Immaculate Conception.

Besides the authority of the theologians, there are two other convincing arguments: first, that she was chosen by God to be the Mother of the divine Word; second, that she was appointed to the office of Mediatrix between God and mankind.

As to the first, Denis the Carthusian asserts that as she was chosen to an order superior to that of all other creatures — the dignity of the Mother of God — so it is reasonable to suppose that from the very beginning of her life gifts of a superior order were conferred upon her, and such gifts as must have incomparably surpassed those granted to other creatures.

And indeed, it cannot be doubted that when the Person of the Eternal Word was, in the divine decree, predestined to make Himself man, a Mother was also destined for Him, from whom

He was to take His human nature. This Mother was the infant whose birthday we celebrate.

St. Thomas Aquinas teaches that: "God gives everyone grace proportioned to the dignity for which He destined him." St. Paul teaches the same thing when he says: "Who also has made us fitting ministers of a new covenant." (2 Cor 3:6) He means that the apostles received gifts from God proportioned to the greatness of the office with which they were charged.

St. Bernardine of Siena adds: "That it is an axiom in theology, that when a person is chosen by God for any state, he receives not only the dispositions necessary for it, but even the gifts which he needs to sustain the state with decorum."

As Mary was chosen to be the Mother of God, it was quite becoming that God should adorn her, in the first moment of her existence, with an immense grace, and one of a superior order to that of all other men and angels, since it had to correspond to the immense and high dignity to which God exalted her.

All theologians come to this conclusion with St. Thomas, who teaches: "The Blessed Virgin was chosen to be the Mother of God; and therefore it is not to be doubted that God fitted her for it by His grace"; so much so that Mary, before becoming Mother of God, was adorned with a sanctity so perfect that it rendered her fit for this great dignity.

The second argument for the sublime graces given to Mary by God is the fact that she has been given the office of Mediatrix. It is well known with what unanimity theologians and Fathers give this title to Mary.

This is because she obtains salvation for all by her powerful intercession and by her merit of "congruity," thereby procuring the great benefit of redemption for the lost world. I say by her merit of congruity, for Jesus Christ alone is our mediator by way of justice and merit in His own right, for He offered His merits to the Eternal Father who accepted them for our salvation.

Mary, on the other hand, is a mediatrix of grace by way of

simple intercession and merit of congruity, she having offered to God, as theologians say with St. Bonaventure, her merits for the salvation of all; God then, as a favor, accepted them with the merits of Jesus Christ.

She effected, as it were, our salvation in union with Christ and thus obtained every gift in the order of grace; and in common with Christ, she bestows these gifts on all.

St. Sophronius, Patriarch of Jerusalem, asserts that the reason for which the Archangel Gabriel called her "full of grace!" was because only limited grace was given to others, but it was given to Mary in all its plenitude. St. Basil of Seleucia declares that she received this plenitude that she might thus be a worthy mediatrix between men and God.

## ii

Now let us pass to the consideration of the second point, that is to say, the greatness of the fidelity with which Mary immediately corresponded to divine grace.

It is the common opinion that this holy child, when she received sanctifying grace at the first instance of her conception in the womb of St. Anne, received also the perfect use of her reason and was divinely enlightened in a degree corresponding to the grace with which she was enriched.

We may well hold that, from the first moment that her beautiful soul was united to her most pure body, by the light she had received from the wisdom of God, she delighted in the eternal truths and rejoiced in all that God had effected in her.

She was free from original sin so she was exempt from every irregular movement, from every distraction, from every opposition on the part of the senses that could stop her progress in advancing more and more in divine love. Her beautiful soul, free from every impediment, never lingered, but always flew towards God, always loved Him, and always increased in love towards Him.

Let us, then, rejoice with our beloved infant who was born so holy, so dear to God, so full of grace. And let us rejoice, not only on her account, but also on our own, for she came into the world full of grace not only for her own glory, but also for our good.

St. Thomas teaches that the most Blessed Virgin was full of grace in three ways:

*First*, she was filled with grace as to her soul, so that from the beginning her beautiful soul belonged to God.

*Second*, she was filled with grace as to her body, so that she merited to clothe the Eternal Word with her own most pure flesh.

*Third*, she was filled with grace for the benefit of all, so that all men might partake of it.

St. Bernard likens her to an aqueduct through which God channels all the graces He sends into the world: "A full aqueduct, that others may receive of her fullness, but not fullness itself."

With what love must we honor her who was first so loved and honored by God!

---

# III
# THE PRESENTATION OF MARY
## *November 21*

### THE OFFERING THAT MARY MADE OF HERSELF TO GOD WAS PROMPT, WITHOUT DELAY AND IT WAS ENTIRE AND WITHOUT RESERVE.

There never was, and never will be, an offering on the part of a pure creature greater or more perfect than that which Mary made to God when, at an early age, she presented herself in the temple to offer Him, not aromatic spices, nor calves, nor gold, but her entire self as a perpetual victim in His honor.

She well understood the voice of God, calling her to devote herself entirely to His love, when he said: "Arise, make haste, my love, my dove, my beautiful one, and come!" (Cant 2:10) She heard the call: "Listen, O daughter, and see, incline your ear; and forget your people and your father's house." (Ps 45:11) She promptly obeyed.

There are two points here for our consideration: Mary's offering was prompt and without delay; second, it was entire and without reserve.

*i*

Mary's offering was prompt. From the first moment that this heavenly child was sanctified in her mother's womb, which was the instant of her Immaculate Conception, she received the perfect use of reason that she might begin to merit. This is the general opinion of the theologians, and particularly Suarez, who says that the most perfect way in which God sanctifies a soul is by its own merit, and as St. Thomas teaches: "To be sanctified by one's own act is the more perfect way. Therefore it is to be believed that the Blessed Virgin was thus sanctified."

From the beginning of her life, Mary knew God and she knew Him in such a way that "no tongue will ever express how clearly this Blessed Mother understood His greatness in that very first moment of her existence," as was revealed to St. Bridget.

This immaculate child understood that her holy parents, Joachim and Anne, had promised God, possibly by vow, that if He granted them issue, they would consecrate it to His service in the temple. Moreover, it was an ancient custom among the Jews to take their daughters to the temple and leave them there for their education.

St. Germanus and St. Epiphanius tell us that at her own volition, she urged her parents to present her to God in the temple. And they, says St. Gregory of Nyssa, "did not long delay in leading her to the temple and offering her to God."

Consider, now, Joachim and Anne, generously sacrificing to God the most precious treasure they possessed in the world, and the one that was dearest to their heart, setting out from Nazareth, and carrying their well-beloved little daughter by turns on the long journey between Nazareth and Jerusalem.

They were accompanied by a few relatives and friends, but also by choirs of angels, as she was about to consecrate herself to the divine Majesty. O how beautiful, how acceptable to God, was every step taken on the way!

There was never a creature so lovely, or so beloved of God, as was Mary when she appeared in the temple to offer herself to Him. When the holy company had reached the temple, the fair child turned to her parents, kissed them and asked their blessing.

Then she ascended the fifteen stairs and presented herself to the priest, St. Zechariah, as St. Germanus tells us. She said farewell to the world and all its pleasures and consecrated herself completely to her Creator.

## ii

The enlightened child knew well that God does not accept a divided heart, but wills that, as He has commanded, it should be consecrated to His love without the least reserve: "You shall love the Lord your God with your whole heart." (Deut 6:5) Therefore, from the first moment of her life she began to love God with all her strength and gave herself entirely to Him.

Still, her most holy soul awaited with the most ardent desire the moment when she might consecrate herself to Him in a more solemn and public way. Let us consider then, with what fervor this loving and tender Virgin gave herself completely to God. In the thought of many authors, it was at this time that she took the vow of virginity, the first ever to do so.

Let us consider how holy was the life that Mary led in the temple. She was like the dawn which rapidly bursts into the full brightness of mid-day, so fast did she grow in perfection. Who can ever describe the always increasing brightness with which her resplendent virtues shone forth from day to day: charity, modesty, humility, silence, mortification, meekness.

St. John Damascene says that she was like a fair olive tree planted in the house of God, and nurtured by the Holy Spirit, she became the dwelling-place of all virtues. According to St. Anselm: "She persevered in prayer, in the study of the sacred Scriptures, in fasting and in all virtuous works."

We read in St. Bonaventure's *Life of Christ* that the Blessed Mother herself revealed to St. Elizabeth of Hungary that: "When her father and mother left her in the temple, she determined to have God alone for her Father, and often thought how she could please Him."

Yes, for the love of this exalted child, the holy Redeemer hastened His coming into the world. In her humility, she longed to be the servant of the Mother of the Messiah, but she herself was chosen for the blessed office of His maternity.

In a word, it was a subject of delight to God to behold this tender Virgin always ascending towards the highest perfection, like a pillar of smoke, rich in the sweet odor of all virtues, perfected in her by the Holy Spirit. When the time came for the Incarnation, as St. Bernard tells us: "There was not on earth a more worthy place than the virginal womb."

As, then, this holy child Mary presented and offered herself to God in the temple with promptitude and without reserve, so let us present ourselves this day to Mary without delay and without reserve; let us entreat her to offer us to God who will not reject us when He sees us presented by the hands of that blessed creature who was the living temple of the Holy Spirit, the delight of her Lord, and the chosen Mother of the Eternal Word.

---

# IV

# THE ANNUNCIATION OF MARY
## *March 25*

IN THE INCARNATION OF THE ETERNAL WORD, MARY COULD NOT HAVE HUMBLED HERSELF MORE THAN SHE DID HUMBLE HERSELF. GOD, ON THE OTHER HAND, COULD NOT HAVE EXALTED HER MORE THAN HE DID EXALT HER.

"Whoever shall exalt himself shall be humbled, and he that humbles himself shall be exalted." (Mt 23:12) These are the words of our Lord, and they cannot fail. Therefore, God having determined to become man, that He might redeem lost sinners and so show the world His infinite goodness, and having to choose a Mother on earth, He sought among women for the one that was the most holy and the most humble.

That special one was the tender Virgin Mary, who, the more exalted her virtues, so much more dove-like was her simplicity and her humility. "There are maidens without number — one alone is my dove, my perfect one." (Cant 6:8-9) Therefore God said: This one shall be my chosen Mother.

Let us now see how great was Mary's humility and consequently how greatly God exalted her.

*i*

Our Lord chose the humble Virgin Mary to be His Mother when He was pleased to become man to redeem the world. But He, for the greater glory and merit of His Mother, would not become her Son without her previous consent.

Therefore, when this humble Virgin (as was revealed to St. Elizabeth of Hungary) was in her little home, sighing and beseeching God more fervently than ever, and with desire more than ever ardent, that He would send the Redeemer; behold, the Archangel Gabriel arrives, the bearer of the great message.

He enters and salutes her: "Hail, full of grace; the Lord is with you; blessed are you among women." (Lk 1:28) Hail, O Virgin full of grace; you were always full of grace above all other saints. The Lord is with you because you are so humble. You are blessed among women, for all others fell under the curse of sin. But you, because you are to be the Mother of the Blessed One, are, and always will be, blessed and free from every stain of sin.

What does the humble Mary answer to a salutation so full of praises? Nothing. She remains silent, but reflecting on it she is troubled: "Who having heard was troubled at his saying, and thought within herself what manner of salutation this might be." (Lk 1:29)

Why was she troubled? Did she fear an illusion, or was it her virginal modesty which caused her to be disturbed at the sight of a man, as some suppose, in the belief that the angel appeared under a human form? No, the text is clear: she was troubled at his saying, not his appearance.

Her trouble, then, arose entirely from her humility, which was disturbed at the sound of praises so far exceeding her own lowly estimate of herself. The more the angel exalted her, the more she humbled herself, and entered into the consideration of her own nothingness.

Here, St. Bernardine remarks: "Had the angel said, 'O

Mary, you are the greatest sinner in the world,' her astonishment would not have been so great; the sound of such high praises filled her with fear."

She was troubled; for, being so full of humility, she abhored every praise of herself, and her only desire was that her Creator, the giver of every good thing, should be praised and blessed.

The Blessed Virgin was already well aware, from the sacred Scriptures, that the time foretold by the prophets for the coming of the Messiah had arrived. The weeks of Daniel were completed. Already, according to the prophecy of Jacob, the sceptre of Judah had passed into the hands of Herod, a stranger king. And Mary knew from prophecy that the Mother of the Messiah would be a Virgin.

She then heard Gabriel give her praises which, it was evident, could apply to no other than to the Mother of God. May not the thought, or at the least some vague impression, have entered her mind that she was this chosen Mother of God? No, her profound humility did not even admit such an idea. These praises only caused great fear in her.

St. Gabriel, seeing Mary so troubled and almost stupified by the salutation, was obliged to encourage her, saying: "Fear not, Mary, for you have found grace with God." (Lk 1:30) Fear not, O Mary, and don't be surprised at the great titles by which I greeted you. If you are so little and lowly in your own eyes, who exalts the humble, has made you worthy to find the grace lost by mankind. He has preserved you from the common stain of the children of Adam.

"The angel awaits your reply," says St. Bernard, "and so do we, O Lady on whom the sentence of condemnation weighs so heavily. We await the word of mercy. See, the price of our salvation is offered to you; we shall be instantly delivered if you consent. For the Lord Himself desires your consent by which He has determined to save the world, with an ardor equal to the love with which He had loved your beauty."

And this is how Mary answers the angel: "Behold the handmaid of the Lord; be it done to me according to your word." (Lk 1:38) O, what more beautiful, more humble, more prudent answer could all the wisdom of men and angels together have invented, had they reflected for a million years?

O powerful answer, which gave joy to heaven and brought an immense sea of graces and blessings into the world! — the answer which had scarcely fallen from the lips of Mary, before it drew the only begotten Son of God from the bosom of His Eternal Father, to become man in her most pure womb!

"Behold the handmaid of the Lord; be it done to me according to your word" when instantly, "the Word was made flesh"; the Son of God became also the Son of Mary. "O powerful *Fiat!*" exclaims St. Thomas of Villanova; "O efficacious Fiat, O Fiat to be venerated! For with a fiat God created light, heaven and earth; but with Mary's fiat God became man, like us."

Consider the great humility of the Blessed Virgin in this answer. She was fully enlightened as to the greatness of the dignity of the Mother of God. She had just been assured by the angel Gabriel that she was this happy Mother chosen by the Lord.

With all this she in no way rises in her own estimation; she does not stop to rejoice in her exaltation. She sees herself as a self-effacing handmaiden in the sight of the majesty of God. St. Bernard in commenting on this remarks: "Though she pleased God by her virginity, she conceived Him by her humility."

As St. Jerome puts it: "God chose her to be His Mother more on account of her humility than all her other sublime virtues." Or as St. Augustine sums up: "Mary's humility became a ladder by which our Lord deigned to descend from heaven to earth."

*ii*

To understand the greatness to which Mary was exalted, it would be necessary to understand the sublimity and the greatness of God. It is actually sufficient to say simply that God made the Blessed Virgin His Mother, to understand that God could not have exalted her more than He did exalt her. God, by becoming the Son of the Blessed Virgin Mary, established her in a rank far above that of all the angels and saints.

With the exception of God Himself, there is no one so greatly exalted. As St. Ephrem asserts: "Her glory is incomparably greater than that of all the celestial spirits." And St. Andrew of Crete says: "God excepted, she is higher than all." As St. Anselm puts it: "No one is equal to you, O Lady, for all are either above or beneath you: God alone is above you, and all that is not God is inferior to you."

We might be surprised that the Evangelists have so much to say in praise of saints like John the Baptizer and the Magdalen, but so little of the precious gifts of Mary. St. Thomas of Villanova remarks: "It was sufficient to say of her, 'Of whom was born Jesus.' What more could they say about the greatness of this Blessed Virgin? It is enough to declare that she is the Mother of God. In these few words they record the greatest, the whole, of her precious gifts."

The reason for this is evident, for as St. Thomas Aquinas teaches: "The nearer a thing approaches its author, the greater is the perfection that it receives from him. Therefore, Mary being of all creatures the closest to God, more than all others, she has partaken of His graces, perfections and greatness."

Therefore the celebrated saying of St. Bonaventure: "To be the Mother of God is the greatest grace that can be conferred on a creature. It is such that God could create a greater world, a greater heaven, but He cannot exalt a creature more than by making her His Mother."

The Blessed Mother probably explains it best when she was inspired by the Holy Spirit to sing out in the Magnificat: "He that is mighty has done great things in me." (Lk 1:49) Why did she not explain these things? Because they are inexplicable.

In conclusion, then, this Blessed Mother is infinitely inferior to God, but immensely superior to all other creatures. As it is impossible to find a Son more noble than Jesus, so it is also impossible to find a Mother more noble than Mary. This reflection should cause the clients of so great a Queen not only to rejoice in her greatness, but should also increase their confidence in her powerful patronage.

Her power to help us is not wanting, neither is her will to help. If we really desire to please her let us often salute her with the "Hail Mary." She once appeared to St. Mechtilde and assured her that she was honored by nothing more than this salutation. By this means we shall certainly obtain even special graces from this Mother of Mercy.

---

# V

# THE VISITATION OF MARY
## *July 2*

MARY IS THE TREASURE OF ALL DIVINE GRACES;
THEREFORE WHOEVER DESIRES GRACES MUST HAVE
RECOURSE TO MARY; AND HE WHO HAS RECOURSE TO
MARY MAY BE SURE OF OBTAINING THE GRACES
HE DESIRES.

Fortunate does that family consider itself which is visited by a royal personage, both on account of the honor that redounds from such a visit, and the advantages that may be hoped for from it. Still more fortunate should that soul consider itself that is visited by the Queen of the world, the most holy Virgin Mary, who cannot but fill with riches and graces those blessed souls whom she deigns to visit.

The house of Obededom was blessed when visited by the ark of God: "And the Lord blessed his house and all that he possessed." (1 Chron 13:14) But with how much greater blessings are those persons enriched who receive a loving visit from this living ark of God, for such was the blessed Mother? How abundantly this was experienced in the home of St. John the Baptizer.

It is for this reason that the feast of the Visitation is often called the feast of Our Lady of Grace. We will consider this holy Mother as the treasure of God's graces and see that all who want heavenly favors must approach her with confidence.

*i*

After the Blessed Virgin had heard from the Archangel Gabriel that her cousin St. Elizabeth had been six months pregnant, she was internally enlightened by the Holy Spirit that the Incarnate Word who had become her Son, wished to impart the first fruits of His graces on that family.

"Mary set out for the hill country with haste. . . ." (Lk 1:39) Rising from the quiet of her contemplation, and leaving the solitude of Nazareth she immediately went on the journey to the home of Elizabeth and Zechariah. As St. Ambrose remarks: "The Holy Spirit does not know slow undertakings."

On entering the house she salutes her cousin. This visit was no ordinary visit such as worldlings conduct, but it was a visit that brought an accumulation of graces. The moment Mary entered the house, Elizabeth was filled with the Holy Spirit; John the Baptizer was cleansed from original sin and sanctified.

These first graces, the first to our knowledge that the eternal Word had granted on earth after His Incarnation, came channeled through Mary. It is quite correct to believe that, from that time on, God made Mary the universal channel, as St. Bernard terms it, through which all the other graces our Lord is pleased to dispense are dispensed.

With reason, then, this holy Mother is called the treasure, the treasurer, and the dispenser of divine grace.

These terms are used by St. Peter Damian, St. Albert the Great, and St. Bernardine. St. Gregory Thaumaturgus observes that: "Mary is said to be so full of grace that in her all the treasures of graces are hidden."

St. Bonaventure, speaking of the field in the Gospel in which a treasure is hidden (Mt 13:44), says that: "Our Queen Mary is this field in which Jesus Christ, the treasure of God the Father, is hid," and with Jesus Christ, is the source and flowing fountain of all graces.

St. Bernard affirms in *De Aquaeductu* that our Lord: "Has deposited the plenitude of every grace in Mary, that we may thus know that if we possess hope, grace, or anything salutary, that it is through her that it came." He concludes: "Let us seek for grace and seek it through Mary, for that which she seeks she finds, for such is the will of God who is pleased to send all through Mary."

*ii*

Because confidence is necessary to obtain graces, we all now consider how sure we ought to feel of obtaining them through the intercession of Mary.

The Church applies these words to Mary on many of her feasts: "With me are riches . . . that I may enrich those who love me." (Prov 8:18-21) The riches of eternal life are kept by Mary for no other reason than to serve us. St. Bernard reminds us that: "Mary is a full aqueduct so that others may receive of her plenitude."

Now that we have this Mother of Mercy, what graces are there that we need fear not to obtain when we cast ourselves at her feet? "I am the city of refuge," St. John Damascene has her say, "for all those who have recourse to me."

Let us then, O devout clients of Mary, rouse ourselves to greater and greater confidence each time that we have recourse to her for favors. That we may do so, let us always remember two great prerogatives of this good Mother: her great desire to do us good, and the power she has with her Son to obtain whatever she asks.

To be convinced of the desire that Mary has to be of service to all, we need only consider the mystery of the present feast: Mary's visit to St. Elizabeth. The journey from Nazareth to Hebron, where many place the home of Zechariah and Elizabeth, was about sixty-nine miles. It was an arduous journey for the Blessed Virgin in her delicate condition, but the charity in her heart would not let her even consider the trouble and the fatigue. She went to be of service and she went quickly, as soon as she heard the message.

And in the chronicle of the Dominican Order, we read the story of Brother Reginald, who was very ill. He devoutly asked Mary to grant him the gift of a return to good health. His sovereign Lady appeared to him in the company of St. Cecilia and St. Catherine and said with great sweetness: "My son, what do you desire from me?" He was so astounded that he did not know what to ask.

Then one of the saints gave him this advice: "Reginald, I will tell you what to do: ask for nothing, but place yourself entirely in her hands, for Mary will know how to grant you a greater grace than you could possibly ask." And the chronicle continues with the witness that Brother Reginald followed this good advice, and was restored to health.

And if we desire the happiness of receiving the visits of the Queen of heaven, we should often visit her by honoring and visiting her shrines and the places of Marian devotion. It is difficult to imagine a Catholic Church that does not have a statue, a picture, or a place devoted to the holy Mother of God.

---

# VI

## THE PURIFICATION OF MARY
### *February 2*

**THE GREAT SACRIFICE WHICH MARY MADE ON THIS DAY TO GOD IN OFFERING HIM THE LIFE OF HER SON.**

In the old law there were two precepts concerning the birth of the first-born sons. One was that the mother should remain as unclean, retired in her house for forty days; after which she was to go to purify herself in the temple. The other was that the parents of the first-born son should take him to the temple, and there offer him to God.

On this day, the most Blessed Virgin obeyed both of these precepts. Although Mary was not bound by the law of purification, since she was always a virgin and always pure, yet her humility and obedience made her wish to go like other mothers to purify herself.

At the same time she obeyed the second precept, to present and offer her Son to the Eternal Father. "And after the days of her purification were accomplished, according to the law of

Moses, they carried Him to Jerusalem to present Him to the Lord." (Lk 2:22)

The Blessed Virgin did not offer Him as other mothers offered their sons. Others offered them to God; but they knew that this oblation was simply a legal ceremony, and that, by redeeming them they made them their own, without fear of again having to offer them to death.

Mary really offered her Son to death; she knew for certain that the sacrifice of the life of Jesus, which she then offered, was one day to be actually consummated on the altar of the cross. So Mary, by offering the life of her Son, came, in consequence of the love she bore this Son, really to sacrifice her own entire self to God.

Leaving aside, then, all other considerations into which we might enter on the many mysteries of this feast-day, we will only consider the greatness of the sacrifice which Mary made of herself to God, in offering Him on this occasion the life of her Son.

The Eternal Father had already determined to save mankind, which was lost by sin, and to deliver them from eternal death. Because He willed at the same time that His divine justice should not be defrauded of a worthy and due satisfaction, He spared not the life of His Son already become man to redeem man, but willed that He should pay with the utmost rigor the penalty which mankind had deserved. "He that spared not even His own Son, but delivered Him up for us all." (Rm 8:32)

He sent Him to earth to become man. He destined Him a Mother, and willed that this Mother should be the Blessed Virgin Mary. But as He willed that His divine Word should not become her Son before she, by an express consent, had accepted Him; so He also willed that Jesus should not sacrifice His life for the salvation of sinful men without the concurrent assent of Mary; that together with the sacrifice of the life of the Son, the mother's heart might also be sacrificed.

From the moment she became the Mother of Jesus, Mary consented to His death, yet God willed that on this day she should make a solemn sacrifice of herself by offering her Son to Him in the temple, sacrificing His precious life to divine justice. St. Epiphanius says she acted "somewhat like a priest."

Now we begin to see how much this sacrifice cost her, and what heroic virtues she had to practice when she herself subscribed the sentence by which her beloved Jesus was condemned to death.

Consider Mary on her journey to Jerusalem to offer her Son. She hastens her steps towards the place of sacrifice and she herself bears the beloved Victim in her arms. She enters the temple, approaches the altar and there, beaming with modesty, devotion and humility, she presents her Son to the Most High.

In the meantime, the holy Simeon, who had received a promise from God that he should not die without having first seen the expected Messiah, takes the divine Child from the hands of the Blessed Virgin, and enlightened by the Holy Spirit, announces to her how much the sacrifice which she then made of her Son would cost her, and that with Him her own blessed soul would also be sacrificed.

St. Thomas of Villanova contemplates some of the dialogue between Mary and Simeon, and he has the holy elder go on to say: "This Child, which is now such a source of joy to you will one day be a source of so bitter grief to you that no creature in the world has ever experienced the like. This will be when you see Him persecuted by men of every class, made a butt for their scoffing and outrages, and even put to death as a criminal, before your very eyes."

Yes, she will suffer in her heart; for compassion alone for the sufferings of this most beloved Son was the sword of sorrow which was to pierce the heart of the Mother, as St. Simeon foretold: "And your very own being a sword shall pierce." (Lk 2:25)

As St. Jerome reminds us, Mary, enlightened by the Holy Spirit, knew very well the prophecies of Scripture which foretold the passion and death of her Son, the Messiah. That He would be betrayed (Ps 41:10), abandoned (Zech 13:7), derided (Is 50:6), scorned (Ps 22:7), scourged (Is 53:2, 5), and crucified (Ps 22:17-18).

Mary, I say, knew all these torments that her Son was to endure, but in the words addressed to her by Simeon, all the minute circumstances of the sufferings, internal and external, that were to torment her Jesus in His Passion, were made known to her, as our Lord revealed to St. Teresa.

She consented to all with a constancy which filled even the angels with astonishment. All this was involved in her sacrificial offering of her Son this day in the temple. She consented completely to the will of God, and the sword was indeed to pierce her heart and soul.

So it is that Mary was silent during the Passion of Jesus when He was unjustly accused. She made no impassioned plea to Pilate, who was of a mind to release Jesus, knowing His innocence. She only appeared in public to assist at the great sacrifice on Calvary. "There stood by the cross of Jesus His Mother" (Jn 19:25), until she saw Him expire and the sacrifice was consummated. All of this she did to complete the offering she had made of Him in the temple.

To understand the violence which Mary had to offer herself in this sacrifice, it would be necessary to understand the love that this Mother bore to Jesus. How ineffable the Son! How noble the Mother! How much it cost her, and how much strength of mind she had to exercise this act, by which she sacrificed the life of so amiable a Son to the cross.

The sufferings of this painful offering did not end in the temple that day. From that time forward, during the whole life of her Son, Mary had constantly before her eyes the death and all the torments that He was to endure. Therefore, the more this Son showed Himself beautiful, gracious and amiable, the more did the anguish of her heart increase.

St. Anselm addresses her: "O most compassionate Lady, I cannot believe that you could have endured for a moment so excruciating a torment without expiring under it, had not God Himself, the Spirit of Life, sustained you."

And St. Bernard affirms, speaking of the great sorrow that Mary experienced on this day, that from that time forward: "She died living, enduring a sorrow more cruel than death." In every moment she lived dying, for in every moment she was assailed by the sorrow of the certain death of her beloved Jesus, which was a torment more cruel than death.

If the sacrifice of Abraham by which he offered his son Isaac to God was so pleasing to the divine Majesty, that as a reward He promised to multiply his descendants as the stars of heaven (Gn 22:16-17) — we must certainly believe that the more noble sacrifice which the great Mother of God made to Him of her Jesus, was far more agreeable to Him, and therefore that He has granted through her prayers the number of the elect should be multiplied by the number of her fortunate children.

At the death of Jesus, Mary united her will to that of Jesus, her Son, so much so, that both offered one and the same sacrifice. It was an offering that grew in Mary's soul, starting with this day in the temple.

# VII
# THE ASSUMPTION OF MARY (I)

HOW PRECIOUS WAS THE DEATH OF MARY, BOTH
ON ACCOUNT OF THE SPECIAL GRACES THAT
ATTENDED IT, AND ON ACCOUNT OF THE MANNER
IN WHICH IT TOOK PLACE.

Death being the punishment of sin, it would seem that the
Blessed Mother — all holy, and exempt as she was from the
slightest stain — should also have been exempt from death, and
from encountering the misfortunes to which the children of
Adam, infected by the poison of sin, are subject.

But God was pleased that Mary should resemble Jesus in all
things, and as the Son died, it was becoming that the Mother
should also die. Moreover, because He wished to give the just an
example of the precious death prepared for them, He willed that
even the most Blessed Virgin should die, but by a sweet and
happy death.

(Editorial Note.   *While most scholars follow this reasoning of St.*
*Alphonsus, there are some who feel that the "dormitio" or "falling*
*asleep of the Virgin" meant that she was preserved by her Son from*
*actual death. It is interesting to note that when Pope Pius XII*
*defined the doctrine of the Assumption on Nov. 1, 1950, he defined*
*that she was taken body and soul into heaven, but he carefully*
*omitted reference to her death. This is still an open question.)*

*i*

There are three things which make death bitter: attachment to the world, remorse for sins, and the uncertainty of salvation. The death of Mary was entirely free from these causes of bitterness, and was accompanied by three special graces which rendered it precious and joyful. She died as she had lived, entirely detached from the things of the world; she died in perfect peace and in the certainty of eternal glory.

I. There can be no doubt that attachment to earthly things makes the death of the worldly bitter and miserable, as the Holy Spirit says: "O death how bitter is the remembrance of you to a man who holds his possessions in peace." (Ec41:1)

But because the saints die detached from the things of this world, their death is not bitter, but sweet, lovely and precious. As St. Bernard remarks, that makes it worth purchasing at any price, however great.

"Blessed are the dead who die in the Lord." (Rev 14:13) Who are they, who, being already dead, die? They are those happy souls who pass into eternity already detached, and, so to speak, dead to all affection for terrestrial things. They are like St. Francis of Assisi who found in God alone all their happiness, and with him could say "My God and my all!"

What soul was ever more detached from earthly goods, and more united to God than the beautiful soul of Mary? She was detached from riches, content to live as a poor woman, supporting herself by the labor of her own hands. She was detached from honors, loving the humble life though the honors due a Queen were hers.

Death for her was not bitter but on the contrary, a very precious thing.

II. Peace of mind makes the death of the just precious. Sins committed during life are the worms that so cruelly torment and gnaw at the hearts of poor dying sinners. They see themselves about to go before the tribunal of God, with their sins clamoring out against them.

Mary certainly could not be tormented at the hour of death by any remorse of conscience since she was free from even the slightest shadow of sin, actual or original. How well it can be said of her: "You are all fair, O my love, and there is not a spot in you." (Cant 4:7)

From the moment of her conception in the womb of St. Anne, she was precious to God. She loved Him and continued to advance in that love throughout her lifetime. "Blessed are the dead who die in the Lord, for their works follow them." (Rev 14:13)

III. Finally, the certainty of eternal salvation makes death sweet, indeed. Death is called a passage, for by it we pass from a short to an eternal life. As the dread of those is indeed great, who die in doubt of their salvation and who approach the solemn moment with well-grounded fear of passing into eternal death; on the other hand, the joy of the saints is indeed great at the close of life hoping with some security to go and possess God in heaven.

When St. Lawrence Justinian was at the point of death, he saw his servants weeping. "Away, away with your tears," he cried, "this is no time to mourn." St. Peter of Alcantara, St. Aloysius Gonzaga and many others, on hearing that death was at hand, burst forth into exclamations of joy and gladness.

What joy, then must the Blessed Mother have felt at the news of her approaching death! She who had the fullest certainty of the possession of divine grace. The Archangel Gabriel had assured her that she was full of grace, and that God was with her. (Lk 1:28)

As divine love gave her life, so did it cause her death, for the Doctors and holy Fathers of the Church generally say that she died of no other infirmity than pure love.

*ii*

Now let us consider how her blessed death took place.

After the ascension of Jesus Christ, Mary remained on earth to attend to the propagation of the faith. The disciples of the Lord could have recourse to her and she could comfort them and encourage them in their work and in the midst of persecutions.

She willingly remained on earth, knowing that it was the will of God and for the good of the Church. However, she could not help but feel pain at being separated from the presence of her beloved Son, who had ascended into heaven. "Where your treasure is, there your heart will be also." (Lk 12:34) Since Mary loved no other good than Jesus, He being in heaven, all her desires were in heaven.

It is piously believed that Mary visited many of the places in the Holy Land where her Son had been. She must have revisited Bethlehem, Nazareth, Gethsemane, and Calvary. Some claim that the Archangel Gabriel visited her shortly before her death to announce her summons to the heavenly court. Would she not aptly reply: "Behold the handmaid of the Lord." (Lk 1:38)

But, behold, Jesus is now come to take His Mother into the kingdom of the blessed. And now death came, not indeed, clothed in mourning and grief, but adorned with light and gladness. Let us say, rather, that divine love came and cut the thread of that noble life.

Mary then has left this world; she is now in heaven body and soul. From there this compassionate Mother looks down upon us who are still in this valley of tears. She pities us and promises to help us. Let us beg her for the grace of a happy death and, if it be the will of God, on a day dedicated to her feasts.

# VIII
# THE ASSUMPTION OF MARY (II)

### HOW GLORIOUS WAS THE TRIUMPH OF MARY WHEN SHE ASCENDED TO HEAVEN — HOW EXALTED WAS THE THRONE TO WHICH SHE WAS ELEVATED

On the Feast of the Assumption, in the Entrance Hymn at Mass, Holy Church bids us rejoice: "Let us all rejoice in the Lord, celebrating a festival in honor of the Blessed Virgin Mary." And justly so: for, if we love our Mother, we ought to congratulate ourselves more upon her glory than on our own private consolation at having lost her presence here on earth.

That we may rejoice in her triumph and be consoled that she has left our presence, consider how glorious was her triumph and how glorious the throne to which she was exalted.

### *i*

After Jesus Christ had completed by His death, the work of our redemption, we can imagine how ardently the angels longed to have Him return to the heavens. We can also imagine them praying for Mary's presence, the living ark who had been sanctified by His presence in her womb.

The ark of the covenant was carried into the city of David with great pomp. How much more was the rejoicing when Mary entered into heaven. Elijah was carried into heaven on the fiery chariot which was, according to some, a group of angels bringing him there.

But more than angels would greet Mary. We can see the whole heavenly court, headed by its King, her Son, going forth to meet her and accompany her there.

St. Bernardine of Siena says that: "Jesus went forth in His glory to meet and accompany her." St. Anselm considers that: "It was precisely for this reason that the Redeemer was pleased to ascend to heaven before His Mother, that is, He did so not only to prepare a throne for her in that kingdom, but also that He might accompany her with all the blessed spirits and so make her entry into heaven more glorious, and such as became one who was His Mother."

Let us consider how our Savior went forth to meet His Mother. Did He say to her: "Come, my own dear Mother, my pure and beautiful dove. Leave the valley of tears in which, for my love, you have suffered so much. Come in soul and body to enjoy the rewards of your life."

Mary leaves the earth at which she looks with affection and compassion: with affection, remembering the many graces she had received there from the Lord; and with compassion, because in it she leaves so many of her poor children surrounded with miseries and dangers.

But see, Jesus offers her His hand, and the Blessed Mother already ascends. Already she has passed beyond the clouds, and she is at the gates of heaven. She passes in to take possession of her kingdom.

And who can this creature be, so beautiful, yet she comes from the desert of earth? She comes pure and rich in virtue, leaning on her beloved Lord, who is graciously pleased to accompany her with such honor. Who is she? The angels sing out: "She is the Mother of our King; she is our Queen, the blessed one among women; full of grace; the saint of saints; the beloved of God; the immaculate one, the fairest of all creatures!"

All the saints in Paradise come to greet her. The virgins salute her as the prime example of consecrated women. The confessors salute her as their mistress, who, by her holy life, taught so many of the virtues. The holy martyrs come to salute her as their Queen, for she, by her constancy in the sorrow of her Son's Passion had taught them to lay down their lives for Christ.

St. James, the only one of the apostles in heaven at the time, comes to thank her in the name of all of them for her comfort and strength while on earth. The prophets are next in line, and then the patriarchs, for she is the glory of their line and the fulfillment of their prophecies.

Adam and Eve are among the number and they thank her with the greatest affection, for she has repaired the injury they inflicted on the human race. And how beautiful was the reunion between her and her parents, St. Joachim and St. Anne, with St. Zechariah and St. Elizabeth, with St. John the Baptizer.

And who can imagine the affection with which she greets her dear spouse, St. Joseph? Who can imagine his joy over the splendid reception Mary receives as she enters heaven?

The humble and holy Virgin adored the divine Majesty, thanking Him for all the graces bestowed on her by His pure goodness, and especially for having made her the Mother of the eternal Word.

And then let him who can, comprehend with what love the Most Holy Trinity blessed her. Think of the welcome extended to His Daughter by the Eternal Father, to His Mother by the Son, to His Spouse by the Holy Spirit.

The Father crowned her by imparting His power to her; the Son, His wisdom; the Holy Spirit, His love. And the three divine Persons, placing her throne at the right of that of Jesus, declared her Sovereign of heaven and earth; and commanded the angels and all creatures to acknowledge her as their Queen, and as such to serve and obey her.

*ii*

Let us now consider how exalted was the throne to which Mary was raised in heaven.

"If the mind of man," says St. Bernard, "can never comprehend the immense glory prepared in heaven by God for those who on earth have loved Him, as the Apostle tells us (1 Cor 2:9), who can ever comprehend the glory that He had prepared for His beloved Mother, who, more than all men, loved Him on earth, indeed, from the first moment of her conception, loved Him more than all men and angels combined?"

And since it is certain that God rewards according to merit, as the Apostle writes, "who will render to every man according to his works" (Rm 2:6), it is also certain, as St. Thomas teaches, that the Blessed Virgin "who was equal to and even superior in merit to all men and angels, was exalted above all the celestial orders."

"In fine," adds St. Bernard, "let us measure the singular grace that she acquired on earth, and then we may measure the singular glory which she obtained in heaven"; for "according to the measure of her grace is the measure of her glory in the kingdom of the blessed."

In each of the saints there were different graces, as St. Paul says: "there are diversities of graces" (1 Cor 12:4). Each of them, by responding to the grace that he had received, excelled in some particular virtue — the one in saving souls, the other in leading a penitential life; one in enduring torments, another in a life of prayer. And as in their merits they differ, so do they differ in celestial glory, for "star differs from star." (1 Cor 15:41) Apostles differ from martyrs, confessors from virgins, the innocent from the penitent.

The Blessed Virgin, being full of all graces, excelled each saint in every particular virtue. She was Queen of the Apostles and Queen of martyrs, who suffered more than all of them; she was the standard-bearer for virgins and the model of the married. She united in her heart all the most heroic virtues that any saint ever practiced.

She possessed them in such a degree, that as "the splendor of the sun exceeds that of all the stars," says St. Basil of Seleucia, "does Mary's glory exceed that of all the blessed." St. Albert the Great confirms it, saying: "Our Queen contemplates the majesty of God in incomparably closer proximity than all other creatures."

Let us, then rejoice with Mary that God has exalted her to so high a throne in heaven. Let us also rejoice on our own account, for although our Mother is no longer present with us on earth, having ascended in glory to heaven, yet in affection she is always with us. In fact, being there nearer to God, she knows our miseries even better and her power to help us is even greater.

Let us then, in the meantime, dedicate ourselves to the service of this Queen, to honor and love her as much as we can.

# PART THREE
# THE SORROWS OF MARY

# THE SORROWS OF MARY

**MARY IS THE QUEEN OF MARTYRS, FOR HER
MATRYDOM WAS LONGER AND GREATER THAN THAT
OF ALL THE MARTYRS.**

Who can ever have a heart so hard that it will not melt on hearing the most lamentable event that once occurred in the world? There was a holy and noble mother who had an only son. That son was the most amiable that can be imagined — innocent, virtuous, beautiful, who loved his mother so tenderly.

Hear, then, what happened. This son, through envy, was falsely accused by his enemies, and, although the judge knew and confessed the son's innocence, that he might not offend his enemies, he condemned him to the ignominious death that they demanded.

This poor mother had to suffer the grief of seeing that lovable and beloved son unjustly snatched from her in the flower of his age by a barbarous death. After immense torments he was made to die on an infamous gibbet in a public place of execution, and this before her own eyes. Is not this event and this unhappy mother worthy of compassion?

You already understand of whom I speak. This son, so cruelly executed, was our loving Redeemer, Jesus; this mother was the Blessed Virgin Mary. For the love that she bore us, she was willing to see Him sacrificed to divine justice by the barbarity of men.

This great torment which Mary endured for us — a torment that was more than a thousand deaths — deserved both our compassion and our gratitude. Let us consider the greatness of the sufferings by which Mary became the Queen of martyrs. The sufferings of her great martyrdom exceeded those of all the martyrs. First, they were the longest in point of duration, and second, in point of intensity.

*i*

As Jesus is called the King of sorrows and the King of martyrs because He suffered during His life more than all other martyrs, so also is Mary called the queen of martyrs, having merited this title by suffering the most cruel martyrdom possible after that of her Son.

That Mary was truly a martyr cannot be doubted. It is an undoubted fact that suffering sufficient to cause death is martyrdom, even though death does not follow. St. John the Evangelist is revered as a martyr even though he did not die in the caldron of boiling oil.

St. Thomas teaches that: "To have the glory of martyrdom, it is sufficient to exercise obedience in its highest degree, that is to say, to be obedient unto death." "Mary was a martyr," says St. Bernard, "not by the sword of the executioner, but by the bitter sorrow of heart."

If her body was not wounded by the hand of the executioner, her blessed heart was transfixed by a sword of grief at the Passion of her Son, grief which was sufficient to cause her death not once, but a thousand times. Not only was it a real death, but her martyrdom surpassed that of all others. Her whole life may be said to have been a prolonged death.

"The Passion of Jesus began at His birth," according to St. Bernard. So also did Mary, in all things like her Son, endure her martyrdom throughout her life. Enlightened by the Holy Spirit, she well understood the prophetic passages that referred to Christ's Passion and death. This was with her from the moment of the Incarnation.

The sword of sorrow predicted by Simeon was with her all her life, as she herself explained to St. Bridget. Well might Mary pray in the words of David: "My life is wasted with grief, and my years in sighs" (Ps 31:11), and, "My sorrow is continually before me." (Ps 38:18) Her heart was always filled with the knowledge of the sufferings of Jesus, and she corresponded to that.

Therefore, time, which usually mitigates the sorrows of the afflicted, did not relieve Mary. Indeed, it rather increased her sorrows. For as Jesus grew and advanced in age and wisdom, so also did the time of His death grow closer. Her martyrdom lasted a lifetime, as it did for her beloved Son.

## ii

Now let us consider the intensity of Mary's martyrdom. Mary is not only the Queen of martyrs because her martyrdom lasted longer than that of all others, but because it is the greatest of all martyrdoms.

Jeremiah seems unable to find anyone with whom he can compare this Mother of sorrows: "To what shall I compare you, or to what shall I liken you, o daughter of Jerusalem? . . . For great as the sea is your destruction; who shall heal you?" (Lm 2:13)

St. Anselm proclaims that: "Had not God by a special miracle preserved the life of Mary in each moment of her life, her grief was such that it would have caused her death." St. Bernardine of Siena goes so far as to say that: "The grief of Mary was so great that, were it divided among all men, it would suffice to cause their immediate death."

We must remember that the martyrs endured their torments, which were the effects of fire or other material agencies, in their bodies; Mary suffered hers in her soul. She was transfixed by the sword of sorrow in the very depths of her being. As the soul is more noble than the body, so much greater were Mary's sufferings than those of all others.

As Jesus Himself told St. Catherine of Siena: "Between the sufferings of the soul and those of the body there is no comparison."

Arnold, the Abbot of Chartres says that: "Whoever had been present on Mount Calvary, to witness the great sacrifice of the Immaculate Lamb of God, would have seen two great altars there, the one in the body of Jesus, the other in the heart of Mary. On that mountain, at the same time the Son sacrificed His body by death, Mary sacrificed her soul by compassion."

St. Antoninus reminds us that while other martyrs suffered by sacrificing their own lives, the Blessed Virgin suffered by sacrificing her Son's life — a life that she loved more than her own. She not only suffered in her soul all that her Son endured in His body, but the sight of her Son's torments brought more grief to her heart than if she had endured them herself, in her own person.

Mary suffered in her heart all the outrages that she saw inflicted on her beloved Jesus. With Him she suffered the tortures, the scourges, the thorns, the nails, the cross. Whatever was inflicted on His innocent body entered at the same time into the heart of Mary to complete her martyrdom.

According to St. Lawrence Justinian, the heart of Mary "became a mirror of the Passion of her Son, in which might be seen, faithfully reflected, the spitting, the blows and wounds and all that Jesus suffered." And St. Bonaventure: "Those wounds which were scattered over the body of Jesus were all united in the single heart of Mary."

Erasmus, speaking of parents in general says that: "They are more cruelly tormented by their children's sufferings than by their own." This may not always be true, but in Mary's case it was evidently so. As St. Bernard comments: "The soul is more where it loves than where it lives." Our Lord had already taught this: "Where our treasure is, there also is our heart." (Lk 12:34)

It is certain that the more we love something, the greater is the pain we feel in losing it. We are more afflicted at the loss of a brother than of a beast of burden. We are more grieved at the loss of a son than at the loss of a friend. To understand the greatness of Mary's grief we must understand the greatness of the love she has for Him.

Who can ever measure the greatness of that love! As St. Amadeus points out: "In the heart of Mary two kinds of love for her Jesus were united — she loved Him with a supernatural love as her God, and natural love by which she loved Him as her Son." And St. Albert the Great adds: "Where there is the greatest love, there is the greatest grief."

So great a love on the part of Mary deserves our gratitude, and that gratitude should be shown by meditating on her sorrows and showing our loving compassion. Those who are devoted to the sorrows of Mary can be assured of great graces from her Son.

*Reflections on each of the Seven Sorrows*
*of Mary*

# I

# ST. SIMEON'S PROPHECY

In this valley of tears every man is born to weep, and all must suffer, by enduring evils which are of daily occurrence. But how much greater would the misery of life be, if we also knew the future evils that await us. "Unfortunately, indeed, would this lot be," says Seneca, "who, knowing the future, would have to suffer it all by anticipation."

Our Lord shows us this mercy. He conceals the trials that await us, so that, whatever they may be, we have to endure them only once.

He did not show this compassion to Mary. She, whom God willed to be the Queen of Sorrows, and in all things like her Son, had to see always before her eyes and continually suffer all the torments that awaited her. These were the sufferings of the Passion and death of her beloved Jesus.

In the temple, St. Simeon took the divine Child in his arms and foretold to her that that Son would be a mark for all the persecutions and opposition of men. "Behold, this Child is set . . . for a sign which will be contradicted." Therefore a sword of sorrow shall pierce her soul: "And your own soul a sword shall pierce." (Lk 2:34-35)

It was revealed to St. Teresa concerning the Blessed Mother, that although she knew her Son the Messiah would suffer greatly, the prophecy of St. Simeon made her aware in greater detail of the cruel death Jesus would endure. She understood then that He would be contradicted in everything and that

His teachings would be declared blasphemy, and He worthy of death (Mt 26:65).

Mary received the announcement that her Son should be persecuted and die with great calmness and peace of soul, for she was always united to the will of God. But, what grief must she have suffered silently, seeing this amiable Son, always near her, hearing from Him words of eternal life and witnessing His holiness of life.

For thirty-three years Mary had to bear this grief. The Blessed Virgin revealed to St. Bridget that there was not an hour on earth in which this grief did not pierce her soul. And as He grew more lovable to her through the years, so did the grief grow as the time for the Passion and death neared.

Since, then, Jesus, our King, and his most holy Mother, did not refuse for love of us, to suffer such cruel pains throughout their lives, it is reasonable that we, at least, should not complain if we have to suffer something.

---

## II

## THE FLIGHT OF JESUS INTO EGYPT

Herod, having heard that the expected Messiah was born, foolishly feared that He would deprive him of his throne. The impious Herod waited to hear from the Magi where the King was born, that he might take His life. Finding himself deceived, he ordered all the infants that could be found in the neighborhood of Bethlehem to be put to death.

Then it was that the angel appeared in a dream to St. Joseph and told him: "Arise and take the Child and His Mother and fly into Egypt." (Mt 2:13) Immediately, on that very night,

St. Joseph informed Mary, and taking the Infant Jesus they set out on their journey.

"O God!" says St. Albert the Great, in the name of Mary, "must He then fly from men, who came to save men?" The afflicted Mother knew that St. Simeon's prophecy was already taking effect. He is no sooner born than He suffers His first persecution.

St. John Chrysostom addresses her: "Flee from your friends to strangers, from God's temple to the temples of devils. What greater tribulation than that a newborn Child, hanging from its Mother's breast, and she too in poverty, should with Him be forced to fly?"

Anyone may imagine what Mary must have suffered on this journey. The journey was great, perhaps three hundred miles, taking, perhaps, a month. Were the roads rough and lightly traveled? Did they join a group of strangers for protection? What a sight, this slight young woman, this Babe a newborn, and St. Joseph their only human protector!

They probably took refuge in the Jewish quarter of some city, such as old Cairo (Memphis) or Heliopolis. It is the opinion of many of the saints that they stayed there about seven years, working hard, in the midst of poverty, to make a decent living.

After the death of Herod, the angel returns in a dream to direct the Holy Family back to the land of Israel (Mt 2:19-23). The reverse journey was probably better planned, without the fear and haste of the former trip, but there must still have been some trepidation at what awaited them there. When they arrived, St. Joseph was hesitant about settling in Judea, and with further angelic guidance he settled his precious family in Galilee, at Nazareth.

The sight, then, of Jesus, Mary and Joseph wandering as fugitives through the world, teaches us that we also must live as pilgrims in this world. We must be detached from the goods which this world offers and which we must soon leave to enter eternity: "We have here no lasting city, but seek one that is to come." (Heb 13:14)

Whoever wishes to feel less the sufferings of this life must go in company with Jesus and Mary, "Take the Child and His Mother." All sufferings become light, and even sweet and desirable, to him who by his love bears this Son and this Mother in his heart.

---

## III

## THE LOSS OF JESUS IN THE TEMPLE

The Apostle St. James says that our perfection consists in the virtue of patience: "And patience has a perfect work, that you may be perfect and entire, failing in nothing." (Jm 1:4) Our Lord, then having given us this Blessed Virgin as a model of perfection, it was necessary that she carry her sorrows with patience and perseverance that we might admire these virtues in her, and strive to imitate her.

He who is born blind feels little the privation of the light of day; but he who once enjoyed it and loses it by becoming blind suffers much. Those unhappy souls, blinded by the mire of the world, have little knowledge of God, and suffer little at not finding Him. On the other hand, one who has been enlightened by celestial light and the love of God and then is deprived of it, grieves bitterly.

Let us see how much Mary must have suffered from this third sword of sorrow, when, having lost her Jesus in Jerusalem for three days, she was deprived of His most sweet presence, accustomed as she was to enjoy it constantly.

As pious Jews, Mary and Joseph made the customary yearly pilgrimage to the temple in Jerusalem. When Jesus was twelve years old, He accompanied them, but He was so taken with the sight of His Father's house that He remained behind when they left. No doubt Mary thought He was with Joseph, and Joseph was sure that He was with Mary.

Now let us imagine the anxiety of this afflicted Mother during the three days she searched for Him. "Have you seen him whom my soul loves?" (Cant 3:3) would have been her constant question? The pain, the grief, the prayers of her heart must have driven her and St. Joseph during that search.

In her other sorrows, she well knew that they were necessary for the Redemption of the human race. Here she must fear that in some way she had failed, had not been worthy of the trust God had given her. Perhaps she had not treasured properly the great gift that had been entrusted to her.

In this sorrow alone does Mary lovingly complain, or expostulate, with Jesus when He was found: "Son, why have you done this to us? Your father and I have sought you sorrowing." (Lk 2:48) She was not reproving Him, but simply expessing the grief proceeding from the great love she had for Him.

This sorrow of Mary should console those who are desolate and no longer enjoy the sweet presence of their Lord as on previous occasions. God withdraws from them for a time, that they might search for Him again with greater fervor. "Learn then, from Mary," says Origen, "to seek Jesus," for in this world we can seek no greater good than Jesus.

# IV

# THE MEETING OF MARY WITH JESUS WHEN HE WAS GOING TO HIS DEATH.

What Mother ever loved her Son as Mary loved Jesus? He was her only Son, raised among so many troubles, a Son who was both so loving and so lovable. He was a Son, who, at the same time that He was her Son, was also her God, who had come to earth to kindle in the hearts of all the fire of divine love. "I have come to cast fire on the earth, and what will I but that it be kindled." (Lk 12:49)

We can only imagine what a flame He must have enkindled in that pure heart of His holy Mother, void as it was of every earthly affection! The blessed Mother herself told St. Bridget that "love had rendered her heart and that of her Son but one."

That whole flame of love was, at the time of the Passion, changed into an ocean of grief when, as St. Bernardine declares: "If all the sorrows in the world were united, they would not equal that of the glorious Virgin Mary."

The greater was her love for Him, the greater was her grief at the sight of his sufferings. This was especially true when she met her Son, already condemned to death, and bearing His cross to the place of punishment. This is the fourth sword of sorrow to pierce her heart.

When the last day arrived before His Passion, did Jesus come to bid farewell to His Mother, perhaps both of them in tears? As Good Friday proceeded, did one after another of the disciples bring her conflicting reports? The scourging? The insults? The house of Caiaphas? The palace of Herod? Pontius Pilate?

How quickly the news came that the unjust and impious Pilate had condemned a known innocent to crucifixion. "And bearing His own cross, He went forth to that place which is called Calvary." (Jn 19:17)

We can see Mary, probably with St. John, hastening along the path, taking a short cut, and positioning herself at a corner where He must pass. As they passed, St. Bernard notes: "The most sorrowful Mother met her most sorrowful Son." Did those standing around insult the Mother along with the Son?

Alas, what a scene of sorrows presented itself to her — the nails, the hammer, the cords, the fatal instruments of the death of her Son, all of which were carried along in front of Him. What a sword must the sound of the trumpet have been to her heart, which proclaimed the sentence pronounced against her Jesus.

She raised her eyes and saw — O God! — a young man covered with blood and wounds from head to foot, a wreath of crowns on His head, two heavy beams on His shoulder. She looked at Him and hardly recognized Him, saying with Isaiah: "and we have seen him and there was no beauty in him." (Is 53:2)

Love revealed Him to her, and what love and fear must have filled her heart. They looked at each other. He wiped the clotted blood from His eyes. The Son looked at the Mother; the Mother looked at the Son. Looks of bitter grief which, as so many arrows, pierced through and through those two beautiful and loving souls.

The Mother would have embraced Him, but the guards thrust her aside with insults. So then, we must proceed with her to Calvary. "Come," says St. John Chrysostom, "let us accompany Mary as she follows the Immaculate Lamb to His death."

# V

# THE DEATH OF JESUS

We are now to witness a new kind of martyrdom — a Mother condemned to see an innocent Son, and one whom she loves with the whole affection of her soul, cruelly tormented and put to death before her own eyes.

"There stood by the cross of Jesus His Mother." (Jn 19:25) St. John believed that in these words he has said enough of Mary's martyrdom. Consider her at the foot of the cross in the presence of her dying Son, and then see if there is any sorrow like her sorrow.

As soon as our agonized Redeemer had reach the Mount of Calvary, the executioners stripped Him of His clothes, and piercing His hands and feet, "not with sharp, but with blunt nails," says St. Bernard, to torment Him the more, they fastened Him on the cross.

Having crucified Him, they planted the cross and so left Him to die. Then Mary drew closer to the cross to be present at His death. St. Bonaventure addresses her: "Indeed, your heart did not think of its own sorrows, but only of the sufferings and death of your dear Son." Not even the fear of death could separate her from her beloved Son.

What a cruel sight! The agony of the Son of God on the cross, the agony of the Mother of God at the foot of the cross!

As Mary revealed to St. Bridget: "My dear Jesus was breathless, exhausted and in His last agony on the cross. His eyes were sunken, half-closed and lifeless; His mouth hanging open; His cheeks hollow and drawn-in; His head had fallen on His breast; His hair was black with blood; His stomach collapsed; His arms and legs stiff; and his whole body covered with wounds and blood."

All of these sufferings of Jesus were also the sufferings of Mary. "Every torture inflicted on the body of Jesus," says St. Jerome, "was a wound in the heart of the Mother." "Whoever was present there on Mount Calvary," adds St. John Chrysostom, "might see two altars on which two great sacrifices were consummated; the one in the body of Jesus, the other in the heart of Mary."

St. Augustine assures us of the same thing: "The cross and the nails of the Son were also those of the Mother; with Christ crucified, the Mother was also crucified." And St. Bernard: "Love inflicted on the heart of Mary the tortures caused by the nails in the body of Jesus." St. Bonaventure agrees: "At the same time that the Son sacrificed His body, the Mother sacrificed her soul."

O Mary! You had to witness the agony of the dying Jesus but you were not allowed to minister to Him. You heard Him exclaim, "I thirst!" but you could not even give Him a drop of fresh water. You would have clasped Him to your body to comfort Him, but you were not allowed to.

Did it not seem as if even His Eternal Father had abandoned Him? "My God, my God, why have you forsaken me?" (Mt 27:46, Ps 22:2) Mary told St. Bridget that these words never departed from her for the rest of her life on earth.

St. Bernard tells us that, at the foot of the cross, Mary lived dying without being able to die: "Near the cross of Christ His Mother stood half-dead; she spoke not; dying she lived and living she died; nor could she die, for death was her very life."

How true, then that Mary cooperated in our redemption by so thoroughly uniting herself to the Passion and death of Jesus Christ.

## VI

# THE PIERCING OF THE SIDE OF JESUS, AND HIS DESCENT FROM THE CROSS.

"O all you who pass by the way, look and see if there is any sorrow like my sorrow." (Lm 1:12)

Mary says to us this day: "Look at me and see if there has ever been in this world a grief like mine, in seeing Him who has all my love torn from me with such cruelty." And yet there is more suffering in store, as the sixth sword pierce her heart.

It is enough to make devout souls weep, for on this Good Friday sorrow is heaped upon sorrow. Now Mary must watch as Jesus, already dead, is pierced in the side by a cruel lance, and then she must receive that dead body into her arms.

That the joy of the following Paschal Sabbath might not be disturbed, the Jews desired that the body of Jesus and the two thieves should be taken down from the crosses. This could not be done until the men were certified as dead. Soldiers came with iron bars to break their legs.

Mary was still weeping over the death of her Son when she saw these armed men advancing towards her Jesus. Did she, perhaps, entreat them to perpetrate no more indignities on her Son? Even as she pleaded, one of the soldiers brandished his lance and pierced the side of Jesus, from which came a flow of blood and water (Jn 19:34).

As was revealed to St. Bridget, that lance pierced the heart of Jesus in two. There came out the last few drops of blood, to show that our Savior was pleased to give His all for us. The injury of the stroke was inflicted on the dead body of Christ, but Mary suffered its pain. He received the insult; she the agony.

Most of the holy Fathers understand this lance to be, literally, the sword foretold to the Blessed Virgin by St. Simeon; a sword, not a material one, but one of grief, which transfixed her blessed soul in the heart of Jesus where it always dwelled.

The afflicted Mother, fearing that still more indignities might be inflicted on the body, entreated Joseph of Arimathea to obtain the body of her Jesus from Pilate. St. Anselm believes that compassion for the Mother softened the heart of Pilate and moved him to grant her the body of the Savior.

Jesus was then taken down from the cross. O most sacred Virgin, after you gave your Son to the world, with so great love, for our salvation, now that world gives Him back to you, but in what a sad state. He was all fair and beautiful, but now there is no beauty in Him.

"How many swords," exclaims St. Bonaventure, "pierced the poor Mother's soul when she received the body of her Son from the cross!" Consider the anguish it would cause any other to receive into her arms the lifeless body of her son. Then, consider this Son, this Mother!

And yet she knew, even in her grief, that it was for His love of sinners that brought Him to this supreme moment, this perfect sacrifice of love. And she joined Him in offering that redemption to the Eternal Father.

But what would she now say to us, if she were still capable of suffering? What would be her grief to see that men, notwithstanding that her Son has died for them, still continue to torment and crucify Him by their sins!

Her message to us would be:

"Return, sinners, return to the wounded heart of my Son. Return as penitents and He will welcome you. Flee from Him, to Him, from the Judge to the Redeemer, from the tribunal to the cross.

"Now that my Son has died for you, it is no longer a time of fear but one of love — a time to love Him, who, to show the love He has for you, was pleased to suffer so much in your place."

---

## VII

## THE BURIAL OF JESUS

And now, the seventh and last sword of sorrow to pierce the heart of Mary is our subject of contemplation.

We return to Calvary to see Mary, with her Son locked in her arms, absorbed in grief. The holy disciples, fearful that the poor Mother might die in grief, approached her to take the body of her Son to take it away for burial.

They did this with gentle and respectful violence, and having prepared the body for burial, they wrapped it in a linen cloth which was already prepared. On this cloth, which is still preserved at Turin, our Lord was pleased to leave to the world an impression of His sacred body.

The disciples then took Him to the tomb. Choirs of angels must have accompanied that body, along with the disciples, the holy women and the afflicted Mother. When they reached the appointed place, Mary would willingly have buried herself there with Him, had such been His will.

Instead, she went into the holy sepulchre and arranged the body with her own hands. Then with one last look, she withdrew while the tomb was sealed with the great stone.

Certainly Mary's heart was buried in that place with the body of her Jesus. "Where your treasure is, there your heart will be." (Lk 12:34) Jesus was her treasure, her whole life, and it remained with Him.

And where, we may ask, are our hearts buried? In creatures — perhaps in mire? And why not in Jesus, who, although He has ascended into heaven, is still pleased to remain on earth, not dead, indeed, but living in the Most Holy Sacrament of the altar; precisely that our hearts may be with Him, and that He may possess them.

Leaving the sepulchre, in her desolation, Mary returned to her own house. "This Mother," says St. Bernard, "went away so afflicted and sad, that she moved many to tears in spite of themselves and wherever she passed all who met her wept."

When she returned home, she gazed on all the familiar things that reminded her of her Jesus. She recalled how she had pressed that precious baby to her bosom at Bethlehem; she remembered His growing years at Nazareth, their mutual affection, their silent looks, and the words of eternal life. She remembered His gracious preaching throughout Galilee and Judea. And then she remembered the cross! And the tomb!

What a night of sorrow! What a Sabbath desolation!

Let us turn to Mary in the words of St. Bonaventure: "O my own sweet Lady, let me weep. You are innocent; I am guilty. Grant that I may weep with you, at least." Mary weeps for love; let us weep in sorrow for our sins, that weeping we may profit from the sacrifice of Christ.

# PART FOUR
## THE VIRTUES OF THE MOST BLESSED VIRGIN MARY

# THE VIRTUES OF THE MOST BLESSED VIRGIN MARY

St. Augustine says that to obtain with more certainty, and in greater abundance the favors of the saints, we must imitate them. Mary, the Queen of the Saints and our principal Advocate with her Son, is also pleased when we do this, so that she can work more efficaciously in us.

Whoever loves, resembles the person loved, or endeavors to become like that person, according to the well-known proverb: "Love either finds or makes its like." St. Sophronius exhorts us to try to imitate Mary, if we love her, because this is the greatest act of honor that we can give her.

St. Bernard reminds us: "Let the child then endeavor to imitate his Mother, if he desires her favor; for Mary, seeing herself treated like a Mother, will treat him as her child."

To imitate Mary, let us consider some of her virtues.

## I

## THE HUMILITY OF MARY

"Humility," says St. Bernard, "is the foundation and guardian of virtues; and with reason, for without it no other virtues can exist in a soul. Should she possess all virtues, all will depart when humility departs." St. Francis de Sales wrote to St. Jane Frances de Chantal: "God so loves humility that whenever He sees it, He is immediately drawn there."

This beautiful and so necessary virtue was unknown in the world; but the Son of God Himself came on earth to teach it by His own example and willed that in that virtue in particular we should endeavor to imitate Him: "Learn of me because I am meek and humble of heart." (My 11:29)

Mary, being the first and most perfect disciple of Jesus Christ in the practice of all virtues, was first also in that of humility, and by it merited to be exalted above all creatures.

The first effect of humility of heart is a lowly opinion of ourselves. It was revealed to St. Matilda that: "Mary always had a humble opinion of herself and even though she saw herself enriched with the greatest graces, she never preferred herself to anyone."

Not, indeed, that Mary considered herself a sinner: for humility is truth, as St. Teresa remarks. Mary knew that she had never offended God. She acknowledged the greatness of God's favors to her to humble herself even more: everything came from the Eternal Father.

The graces that helped her appreciate the infinite greatness and goodness of God also helped her recognize the lowliness of creatures. St. Bernardine reminds us that: "The Blessed Virgin had always the majesty of God and her own nothingness present to her mind." And he adds: "After the Son of God, no creature in the world was so exalted as Mary, because no creature in the world ever humbled itself so much as she did."

A soul that is truly humble does not praise itself, and when praised by others, refers all to God. When Mary was praised by St. Gabriel the Archangel and later by St. Elizabeth, Mary refers it all to God: "My soul magnifies the Lord; my spirit rejoices in God my Savior." (Lk 1:46 ff.)

There can be no doubt, as St. Gregory of Nyssa remarks, that of all virtues there is perhaps none the practice of which is more difficult to our nature, so wounded by pride and other sins, than that of humility. There is no escape: we can never be true children of Mary if we are not humble. "If," says St. Bernard, "you cannot imitate the virginity of this humble Virgin, imitate her humility."

---

# II

## MARY'S CHARITY TOWARDS GOD

St. Anselm says that: "Wherever there is the greatest purity, there is also the greatest charity." The more a heart is pure, and empty of itself, the greater the fullness of its love towards God.

The most holy Mary, because she was so humble, and had nothing of self in her, was filled with divine love so that: "Her love towards God surpassed that of all men and angels," as St. Bernardine writes. therefore, with reason, St. Francis de Sales called her "the Queen of Love."

God has indeed given us the precept: "You shall love the Lord your God with your whole heart." (Mt 22:37) but, as St. Thomas notes, this will be fulfilled perfectly in heaven, imperfectly in this world. However, his teacher, St. Albert the Great notes that if it has been fulfilled perfectly in this world, it would be by the Blessed Mother. And it was, because the Mother of our Emmanuel practiced virtues in their highest perfection.

In her, the love of God was so ardent that no defect of any kind could have access to her. "Divine love," says St. Bernard, "so penetrated and filled the soul of Mary, that no part of her was left untouched; so that she loved with her whole heart, with her whole soul, with her whole strength, and was full of grace."

God who is love (1 Jn 4:8) came on earth to enkindle the flame of His divine love, but in no heart did He enkindle so much as in that of His Mother. Her heart was pure, that is, entirely free from all earthly affections and entanglements and therefore fully prepared to burn with this fire of love.

St. Ildephonsus remarks that: "The Holy Spirit heated, inflamed and melted Mary with love, as fire does iron." St. Thomas of Villanova says that the bush seen by Moses (Ex 3:2), which burnt without being consumed, was a real symbol of Mary's heart.

St. Bernard applies the words of St. John to her: "And there appeared a great wonder in the heavens, a woman clothed with the sun"(Rev 12:1); for, he writes: "She was so closely united to God by love, and penetrated so deeply the abyss of divine wisdom . . . no creature could have a closer union with Him."

In the opinion of Suarez: "The acts of perfect charity formed by the Blessed Virgin in this life were without number; for nearly the whole of her life was spent in contemplation, and in that state she constantly repeated acts of love." In fact, Mary did not so much repeat acts of love as other saints do, but her whole life was one continued act of love. By a special privilege she always actually loved God.

St. Peter Damian says that: "The duties of her active life did not prevent her from loving, and love did not prevent her from attending to those duties." And St. Ambrose adds: "While her body rested, her soul watched."

Since Mary loved God so much, there can be nothing that she so much requires in her clients as that they also should love God to their utmost. This was the very message she delivered to such privileged souls as St. Bridget and Blessed Angela of Foligno.

"Mary, Queen of love, of all creatures the most amiable, the most beloved," as St. Francis de Sales prayed, "You were always and in all things inflamed with the love of God. Pray that your Son will bestow a spark of that love in my soul."

---

## III

# MARY'S CHARITY TOWARDS HER NEIGHBOR

Love towards God and love towards our neighbor are commanded the same precept: "And this commandment we have from God, that he who loves God loves also his neighbor." (1 Jn 4:21) — St. Thomas says that the reason for this is that one who loves God loves all that God loves.

Since there never was and never will be anyone who loved God as much as Mary loved Him, so there never was and never will be anyone who loved her neighbor as much as she did.

So great was Mary's charity when on earth, that she helped the needy without even being asked. This was the case at the marriage feast of Cana, when she told her Son that family's distress: "They have no wine" (Jn 2:3), and asked Him to work a miracle.

With what speed she hastened to help her elderly cousin, St. Elizabeth, as soon as she heard of her condition and knew she needed help. "She went with haste into the hill-country." (Lk 1:39)

She could not, however, more fully display the greatness of her charity than she did in the offering which she made of her Son to death for our salvation. St. Bonaventure applies these words to Mary: "Mary so loved the world as to give her only-begotten Son."

"Nor has this love of Mary for us diminished," says St. Bonaventure, "now that she is in heaven, but it has increased, for now she sees better the miseries of mankind." He continues: "Great was the mercy of Mary towards the wretched when she was still in exile on earth; it is far greater now that she reigns in heaven."

Blessed is he, says the holy Mother, who listens to my instructions, pays attention to my charity and, in imitation of me, exercises it himself towards others. St. Gregory Nazianzen assures us that: "There is nothing by which we can, with greater certainty, gain the affection of Mary than by charity towards our neighbor."

Therefore, as our Lord exhorts us: "Be merciful as your heavenly Father is merciful." (Lk 6:36) Mary seems to be saying the same to her children. It is certain that our charity towards our neighbor will be the measure of that which God and Mary will show us."Give and it will be given to you . . . for the measure with which you measure will be measured out to you." (Lk 6:38)

St. Methodius used to say: "Give to the poor and receive paradise." St. John Chrysostom put it this way:"Anyone who assists the needy makes God his debtor."

O Mother of Mercy, obtain for me the grace to imitate you in holy charity, both towards God and my neighbor.

---

# IV

# MARY'S FAITH

As the Blessed Virgin is the mother of holy love and hope, so also is she the mother of faith. And with reason is she so, says St. Irenaeus, for: "The evil done by Eve's incredulity was remedied by Mary's faith."

This is confirmed by Tertullian who says that because Eve, contrary to the assurance she had received from God, believed the serpent, she brought death into the world; but our Queen, because she believed the angel, brought life into the world.

St. Augustine writes that: "When Mary consented to the Incarnation of the Eternal Word, by means of her faith she opened heaven to mankind." On account of her faith St. Elizabeth called her blessed: "Blessed are you who have believed, because those things shall be accomplished in you that were spoken by the Lord." (Lk 1:45))

St. Augustine adds that Mary was more blessed by receiving the faith of Christ than by conceiving the flesh of Christ. Suarez takes that up, telling us that the holy Virgin had more faith than all men and angels. She saw the Infant in the crib of Bethlehem and believed Him to be the Creator of the world.

She saw Him fly from Herod and believed Him the King of kings. She saw Him born and believed Him eternal. She saw Him poor and in need and believed Him the Lord of the universe. She heard Him weep and believed Him the joy of paradise. She saw Him in death, despised and crucified, and her faith remained firm that He was God.

On these words in the Gospel: "There stood by the cross of Jesus His Mother" (Jn 19:25), St. Antoninus says: "Mary stood supported by her faith, which she retained firm in the divinity of Christ." St. Albert the Great tells us that: "Mary then exercised perfect faith, for even when the disiciples were doubting, she did not doubt."

Mary merited by her great faith to become "the light of all the faithful," as St. Methodius calls her. St. Cyril of Alexandria calls her "Queen of the true faith." In the Office for Mary, the holy Church prays: "Rejoice, O Virgin Mary, for you alone have destroyed all heresies throughout the world."

St. Ildephonsus exhorts us to imitate Mary's faith, but how can we do this? Faith, at the same time that it is a gift, is also a virtue. It is a gift of God alone, inasmuch as it is a light infused by Him into our souls; and a virtue, inasmuch as the soul has to exercise itself in the practice of it.

Therefore, faith is not only to be the rule of our belief, but also that of our actions. St. Gregory the Great says: "He truly believes who puts what he believes into practice." And St. Augustine: "You say, I believe; do what you say and it is faith." This is to have a lively faith, to live according to our belief. St. James decrlares it thus: "Faith without works is dead." (Jm 2:26)

God searches among the faithful for Christians who have good works, and they seem few. Many have only the name Christian. As Alexander once addressed a cowardly soldier also named Alexander: "Either change your name or change your conduct."

Let us entreat this powerful Mother to obtain for us a faith come alive by charity.

---

# V

# MARY'S HOPE

Hope takes its start from faith; for God enlightens us by faith to know His goodness and the promises He has made, that by this knowledge we may rise by hope to the desire of possessing Him. Mary, then, having had the virtue of faith in its highest degree, had also hope in the same degree of excellence. "It is good for me to adhere to my God, to put my hope in the Lord God." (Ps 73:28)

Mary was indeed that faithful spouse of the Holy Spirit of whom it was said: "Who is she who comes up from the desert, flowing with delights, leaning on her beloved?" (Cant 8:5) For she was always perfectly detached from earthly affection, looking through the world as a desert, and therefore in no way relying either on creatures or on her own merit; but relying only on divine grace, in which was all her confidence, she always advanced in the love of God.

The most holy Virgin gave a clear indication of the greatness of her confidence in God, in the frist place, when she saw the anxiety of her holy spouse St. Joseph. Unable to account for her wonderful pregnancy, he was troubled at the thought of leaving her; "but Joseph was minded to put her away privately." (Mt 1:19)

It appeared then necessary that she should uncover the hidden mystery to St. Joseph; but no, she would not herself manifest the grace she had received. She thought better to abandon herself to divine Providence in the full confidence that God Himself would defend her innocence and reputation.

Mary again showed her confidence in God when she knew that the time for the birth of our Lord approached, and was yet driven even from the lodging of the poor in Bethlehem, and obliged to give birth in a stable: "And she laid Him in a manger, because there was no room for Him in the inn." (Lk 2:7) She placed her confidence in God, knowing that He would assist her.

We see this over and over again in the Gospel account. Her trust in divine Providence during the flight into Egypt and her trust in her Son when, at Cana, she told Him simply: "They have no wine." Her last recorded words in the Scriptures reflect that hope: "Whatever my Son tells you to do, do." (Jn 2:3)

Let us, then, learn from Mary to have that confidence in God which we ought always to have, but principally in the great affair of our eternal salvation — an affair in which it is true that we must cooperate; yet it is from God alone that we must hope for the grace necessary to obtain it. We must distrust our own strength and say with the Apostle: "I can do all things in Him who strengthens me." (Ph 4:13)

Mary, Mother of holy Hope, after Jesus and in Jesus, I place my trust in you.

---

# VI

## MARY'S CHASTITY

Since the fall of Adam, the senses being rebellious to reason, chastity is of all the virtues the one that is the most difficult to practice. St. Augustine calls chastity one of our most difficult daily battles. May God be ever praised, however, since in Mary He has given us a great example of this virtue.

"With reason," says St. Albert the Great, "is Mary called the Virgin of virgins; for she, without the counsel or example of others, was the first who offered her virginity to God." St. Bernard asks: "O Virgin, who taught you to please God by virginity, and to lead an angel's life here on earth?"

St. Sophronius replies: "God chose this most pure Virgin for His Mother, that she might be an example of chastity to all." Therefore St. Ambrose calls her "the standard-bearer of virginity."

St. Jerome declared that it was his opinion that St. Joseph remained a virgin living with Mary. Writing against the heretic Helvidius, who denied Mary's virginity, he says: "You say that Mary did not remain a Virgin. I say that not only she remained a Virgin, but even that St. Joseph preserved his virginity through Mary."

In the struggle to be chaste, St. Robert Bellarmine lists three means: fasting, the avoidance of dangerous occasions, and prayer.

1. By fasting he means mortification of the eyes and of the appetite. It is interesting to note how many stories the

writers pass down concerning the modesty of Mary, her custody of the eyes, and her moderation with food.

St. Gregory of Tours affirms that Mary fasted throughout her life. St. Bonaventure observes that: "Mary would never have found so much grace, had she not been most moderate in her food, for grace and gluttony cannot subsist together."

2. The second means is to fly the occasions of sin. St. Philip Neri says that "in the war of the senses, cowards conquer." Knowing as we do of Mary's complete sinlessness, nevertheless we can be sure that she never dallied with the occasions of sin. There is serious question among the scripture scholars as to whether Mary remained with St. Elizabeth for the actual birth of St. John the Baptizer, questioning the propriety of the young maiden being present.

3. The third means is prayer. "And as I knew," said the wise man, "that I could not otherwise be continent except God gave it . . . I went to the Lord and begged Him for it." (Ws 8:21) The Blessed Virgin revealed to St. Elizabeth of Hungary that she acquired no virtue without effort and continual prayer. John of Avila used to say that: "Many have conquered impure temptations only by having devotion to the Immaculate Conception."

---

# VII

## MARY'S POVERTY

Our most loving Redeemer, that we might learn from Him to despise the things of this world, was pleased to be poor on earth.

"He, although rich, became poor for your sake, that through His poverty you might become rich." (2 Cor 8:9) Therefore our Lord issues this invitation: "If you would be perfect, go, sell what you have and give it to the poor . . . and come, follow me." (Mt 19:21)

Now consider Mary, His most perfect disciple, who indeed imitated His example. Some authors even are of the opinion that Mary made a vow of poverty. She revealed to St. Bridget that: "From the beginning I vowed in my own heart that I would never possess anything on earth."

The gifts received from the holy Magi cannot certainly have been of small value, but it was St. Bernard's opinion that Mary gave them to the poor through the hands of St. Joseph. (Others think these were a providential aid for the flight into Egypt.)

At the presentation of the Child in the temple, Mary and Joseph offered the traditional sacrifice of the poor: "And to offer a sacrifice, according as it was written in the law of the Lord, a pair of turtle-doves or two young pigeons." (Lk 2:24)

Out of love for poverty she did not disdain to marry St. Joseph, who was only a poor carpenter and afterwards to help with the work of her hands, as St. Bonaventure assures us. In a word, she lived poor and she died poor.

St. Philip Neri used to say that: "He who loves the things of the world will never become a saint." We may add the opinion of St. Teresa of Avila on the subject, that: "It justly follows that he who runs after perishable things should also himself be lost." On the other hand, she adds, that the virtue of poverty is a treasure which comprises in itself all other treasures.

Note she says the "virtue of poverty," for, as St. Bernard remarks, this virtue does not consist only in being poor, but in loving poverty. That is why our Lord said: "Blessed are the poor in spirit, for theirs is the kingdom of heaven." (Mt 5:3) They are blessed because they desire nothing but God; in poverty they find their paradise on earth, as St. Francis of Assisi did when he exclaimed: "My Lord and my all."

Let us then, as St. Augustine exhorts us, "love that one good in which all goods are found," and address our Lord in the words of St. Ignatius Loyola: "Give me only your love, with your grace, and I am rich enough." "When we have to suffer from poverty, let us console ourselves," says St. Bonaventure, "with the thought that Jesus and His Mother were also poor like ourselves."

Ah, my most holy Mother, you indeed had reason to say that in God was your joy: "and my spirit has rejoiced in God my Savior." (Lk 1:47) In this world you loved and desired no other good but God. O Lady, detach me from the world that I may love Him alone, who alone deserves to be loved.

---

# VIII

## MARY'S OBEDIENCE

When the Archangel Gabriel announced to Mary God's great designs for her, she, through love of obedience, would only call herself a handmaid: "Behold the handmaid of the Lord." (Lk 1:38) "Yes," remarks St. Thomas of Villanova, "for this faithful handmaid never, in either thought or word or deed, contradicted the Most High; but, entirely despoiled of her own will, she lived always and in all things obedient to that of God."

She herself declared that God was pleased with her obedience, when she said: "He has regarded the humility of his handmaid" (Lk 1:48); for it is in prompt obedience that the humility of a servant properly speaking consists. St. Irenaeus reminds us that: "As Eve by her disobedience caused her own death and that of the whole human race, so did the Virgin Mary, by her obedience, become the cause of her own salvation and of that of all mankind."

Mary's obedience was much more perfect than that of all the other saints, since all men, on account of original sin, are prone to evil, and find it difficult to do good; but not so Mary. According to St. Bernardine: "Because Mary was free from original sin, she found no obstacle in obeying God; she was like a wheel which was easily turned by every inspiration of the Holy Spirit."

"Therefore," continues the same saint, "her only object in this world was to keep her eyes constantly fixed on God, to discover His will, and when she had found out what He required, to perform it."

Mary well proved how ready she was to obey in all things, in the first place, when, to please God, she obeyed even the Roman emperor and undertook the long journey to Bethlehem, in the winter, when she was pregnant, and in such poverty that she had to give birth to her Son in a stable.

She showed equal obedience on undertaking, on the very same night on which she had notice of it from St. Joseph, the longer and more difficult journey into Egypt. The notice was delivered to St. Joseph that Mary might have the merit of obeying him, as well.

But above all, she showed her heroic obedience when to obey the divine will, she offered her Son to death; and this with such constancy as to amaze the saints.

Therefore, St. Bede the Venerable, explaining our Lord's answer to the woman spoken of in the Gospel, who exclaimed, " 'Blessed is the womb that bore you and the breasts that nursed you' . . . 'But more blessed are they who hear the word of God and keep it.' " (Lk 11:27), says that Mary was indeed blessed in becoming the Mother of God, but that she was much more so in always loving and obeying the divine will.

For this reason, all who love obedience are highly pleasing to the Blessed Virgin. She once appeared to a Franciscan friar in his cell. While she was present, obedience called him to hear the confession of a sick person. He went, and on his return found that Mary had waited for him, and highly commended his obedience. On the other hand, she greatly blamed another religious who remained to finish some private devotions after the refectory bell had rung.

The Mother of God herself revealed to St. Bridget that through the merit of her obedience she had obtained so great power that no sinner, however great were his crimes, who had recourse to her with a purpose of amendment, failed to obtain pardon.

Our own sweet Queen and Mother, intercede with Jesus for us. By the merit of your obedience obtain for us that we may be faithful in obeying His will.

---

# IX

## MARY'S PATIENCE

This world being a place of merit, is rightly called a valley of tears; for we are all placed in it to suffer, that we may, by patience, gain for our souls life eternal, as our Lord Himself says: "In your patience you shall possess your souls." (Lk 21:19)

God gave us the Blessed Virgin Mary as a model of all virtues, but more especially as an example of patience. St. Francis de Sales, among others, remarks that it was precisely for this reason that at the marriage-feast of Cana, Jesus Christ gave the Blessed Virgin an answer by which He seemed to value her prayers as little.

He did this that He might give us the example of the patience of His most holy Mother. But then, Mary's whole life was a continual exercise of her patience. Compassion alone for the Redeemer's suffering suffice to make her a martyr of patience.

We have already seen her sorrows, suffering and patience in the flight into Egypt, the hidden life at Nazareth and during her presence at the crucifixion. Then it was that precisely by the merit of her patience, as St. Albert the Great says, she brought us forth to the life of grace.

If we wish to be children of Mary, we must try to imitate her patience. "For what," says St. Cyprian, "can enrich us with greater merit in this life, and greater glory in the next, than the patient enduring of sufferings?"

It is also patience that makes saints, bearing in peace, not only the crosses which come immediately from God, such as sickness and poverty, but also those that come from men — persecutions, injuries, calumnies and the rest.

"Rejoice then," exclaims St. Gregory the Great; "we can be martyrs without the executioner's sword, if only we have patience." "Provided only," adds St. Bernard, "that we endure the afflictions of this life with patience and joy." O what fruit will not every pain borne for God's sake produce for us in heaven! Therefore the Apostle encourages us: "For this momentary light affliction is producing for us an eternal weight of glory far beyond all comparison." (2 Cor 4:17)

When our crosses weigh heavily on us, let us have recourse to Mary who is called by the Church, "the Comfortress of the afflicted," and by St. John Damascene, "the Remedy for all sorrows of the heart."

O Blessed Lady, you were innocent and yet suffered with such patience. Help me, so deserving of sufferings, to bear my crosses with patience.

## X

# THE SPIRIT OF PRAYER AND MEDITATION IN MARY

There was never a soul on earth that practiced in so perfect a manner as the Blessed Virgin the great lesson taught by our Savior: "That we ought always to pray, and not to faint." (Lk 18:1)

From no one, says St. Bonaventure, can we better take example and learn how necessary is perseverance in prayer, than from Mary. St. Albert the Great asserts that, after Jesus Christ, the blessed Mother was the most perfect in prayer of all who ever have been or ever will be.

In the very first moment, in which she had the perfect use of reason, in the first moment of her existence, she began to pray. When as a young child in the temple, she told St. Elizabeth of Hungary, "she always rose at midnight and went before the altar of the temple to offer her supplications."

After the Resurrection and the Ascension, we are told that she frequently visited the places of our Lord's Nativity, Passion and Sepulchre. Moreover, she prayed with the greatest recollection of spirit, free from every distraction and inordinate affection, nor did any exterior occupation ever obscure the light of her unceasing contemplation, as we are assured by Denis the Carthusian.

Indeed, O Mary, there had never been one like you before, nor will there ever be. You alone of women have, above all, pleased Christ.

# PART FIVE

## PRACTICES OF DEVOTION IN HONOR
## OF THE BLESSED MOTHER

# PRACTICES OF DEVOTION IN HONOR OF THE BLESSED MOTHER

"The Queen of Heaven is so gracious and liberal," says St. Andrew of Crete, "that she recompenses her servants with the greatest munificence for the most trifling devotion." However, there are two conditions:

*First.* When we offer her our devotions our souls should be free from sin. Otherwise she would address us as she addressed a wicked soldier spoken of by St. Peter Celestine.

Every day this soldier performed some devotion in honor of our Blessed Lady. One day he was suffering greatly from hunger when Mary appeared to him and offered him some of the most delicious meats, but on so filthy a plate that he could not bring himself to taste them.

"I am the Mother of God," she said, "and I have come to satisfy your hunger." "But, O Lady," he replied, "I can not eat off such a dirty plate." "And how," responded Mary, "can you expect me to accept your devotions, offered from your soul which is so defiled with sin?"

The soldier was converted and became a hermit. Thirty years later, at his death, the Blessed Virgin appeared and took him to heaven.

In the first part of this book we said that it is morally impossible for a client of Mary to be lost. This must be understood on condition that he lives either without sin, or, at least, with the desire to abandon it. Then the Blessed Mother will help him. On the other hand, should anyone sin in the hope that Mary will save him, he would thereby render himself unworthy and incapable of her protection.

*Second.* Perseverance in devotion to Mary is important. "Perseverance alone will merit a crown," says St. Bernard. When St. John Berchmans was dying, his Jesuit companions crowded around the youth and asked him what devotion they should perform that would be most agreeable to our Blessed Lady. He replied: "Any devotion, however small, provided it is constant."

Anyone who perseveres in his devotion to Mary will be blessed in his confidence and will obtain all that is desired. But as no one can be certain of this perseverance, no one before death can be certain of salvation.

Therefore, I now give, with simplicity, and in a few words, some of the various devotions we can offer our Mother to gain her favor. I consider this the most useful section of the book. I do not recommend that you practice them all, but that you pick and choose which one or ones you like, and then practice that constantly.

\* \* \* \* \* \* \* \* \* \*

# I

## THE HAIL MARY

This angelic salutation is most pleasing to the ever-blessed Virgin. Whenever she hears it, it would seem as if the joy which she experienced when St. Gabriel announced to her that she was the chosen Mother of God, is renewed in her.

With this in view, we should often salute her with the "Hail Mary." "Salute her," says Thomas a Kempis, "with the angelic salutation, for she indeed hears this sound with pleasure." The blessed Mother herself assured St. Matilda that no one could salute her in a manner more agreeable to herself than with the "Hail Mary."

St. Bernard was in the custom of saying this whenever he passed a statue or picture of the Blessed Mother. One day, he heard her return the salutation with "Hail, Bernard." St. Bonaventure reminds us that: "She willingly salutes us with grace, if we willingly salute her with a Hail Mary."

*To Practice This Devotion:*

1. We can say every morning and evening, on rising and going to bed, prostrate or kneeling, a Hail Mary. We can add some invocation as well, such as: "O Mary conceived without sin, pray for us who have recourse to you." It is well to have a beautiful picture or statue of the Blessed Virgin.
2. We can say the "Angelus" with the usual invocations and the repetition of the three Hail Marys in the morning, mid-day and evening. St. Charles Borromeo used to stop whatever he was doing to respond to the Angelus bell.
3. Some like to begin each hour with the Hail Mary, whenever the clock strikes the new hour. This was a favorite practice of St. Alphonsus Rodriguez.
4. In leaving and returning home, we can regularly offer a Hail Mary.
5. We should reverence every image of Mary that we pass, with a Hail Mary, If we can, we might provide a wayside or outdoor shrine to our Lady.
6. We can begin and end all of our actions with a Hail Mary.
7. Mary told St. Jane Frances de Chantal that it was a very pleasing practice to her for one to recite ten Hail Marys in honor of her ten virtues.

\*   \*   \*   \*   \*   \*   \*   \*   \*   \*

# II
# NOVENAS

Devout clients of Mary are all attention and fervor in celebrating the novenas, or nine days of prayers preceding the principal feasts of the Blessed Mother; she is all love in dispensing innumerable and most special graces to them. These devotions may be used:

1. We may make mental prayer on the morning and evening, plus a visit to the Blessed Sacrament, adding nine times the "Our Father, Hail Mary and Glory be to the Father."

2. We may pay three visits to a shrine or picture of Mary and thank God for the graces He has given her, each time asking the Blessed Virgin for some special grace.

3. We may make many acts of love to Jesus and Mary throughout the day.

4. Every day of the novena we may read some book about the Blessed Mother and her glories.

5. We can perform some external mortification and also we can fast and abstain. This is particularly valuable on vigils of the feasts. Acts of internal mortification are even more valuable: silence, curbing curiosity or impatience, practicing a special virtue, avoiding entertainment in favor of solitude, etc.

6. Receive Holy Communion frequently during the novena, and especially on the feastday.

7. Choose a special feast of our Lady for your own particular devotion and renew yourself in her service annually.

\* \* \* \* \* \* \* \* \*

## III

## THE ROSARY

Blessed Alan de la Roche gave us the Rosary in its present-day form, but attributed it to the spiritual legacy of St. Dominic. It has been highly approved by many Popes and has stood the test of time as a devotion that is highly conducive to the spiritual life.

The practice in our time is to use the Joyful Mysteries on Monday and Thursday, the Sorrowful Mysteries on Tuesday and Friday, and the Glorious Mysteries on Wednesday and Saturday. On Sundays the liturgical season should be followed, or the Glorious Mysterious used.

Many devout clients of Mary try to recite all fifteen Mysteries every day. Most popular prayer books will have suggestions on various meditations for the Mysteries, if some variety is desired. It is also an accepted practice to use other scenes from the life of our Lord and our Lady in the Mysteries, e.g. the Beatitudes, St. Peter walking on the water, the conversion of St. Paul, etc.

Similarly, the Little Office of the Blessed Virgin, said to have been composed by St. Peter Damian, is a devotion that is very dear to Mary.

And in this category I highly recommend the Litany of Loretto (The Litany of Our Lady).

\* \* \* \* \* \* \* \* \*

## IV

## FASTING

There are many devout clients of Mary who, to honor her, fast on bread and water on Saturdays and on the vigils of her feasts.

According to St. Bernard, Saturdays are set aside for our Lady because on Saturday, the day after the death of her Son, Mary remained steadfast in faith, despite her sorrow and desolation. St. Charles Borromeo promoted and practiced this form of devotion.

Every Saturday we should try to perform some act of devotion in honor of the Blessed Mother, especially attending Mass and receiving Holy Communion.

\* \* \* \* \* \* \* \* \*

# V

## VISITING SHRINES AND PICTURES OF MARY

Holy Church has always defended the use of pictures and statues in our spiritual lives. This is particularly true in devotion to the Blessed Mother, and she has been singularly responsive to visits to her shrines, both the well-known ones and the simple home shrines.

Lights and flowers to decorate these places of devotion have always been popular with Mary's clients. Pilgrimages and processions are also a commendable practice.

\* \* \* \* \* \* \* \* \*

# VI

## THE SCAPULAR

As men esteem it an honor to have persons who wear their livery or uniforms, so also is our Blessed Lady pleased that her clients should wear her scapular as a mark that they have dedicated themselves to her service, and that they are members of the household of God.

One of the most popular scapulars is that of Our Lady of Mount Carmel, which is attributed to our Lady herself, who gave it to St. Simon Stock in 1251. There are several other scapulars approved by the Church, such as that of the Immaculate Conception, the Seven Sorrows, and the Holy Trinity.

(*Editorial Note.* Since World War I, the Popes have allowed the cloth scapulars to be replaced with medals, and there are many which combine four or more scapulars on one medal.)

\* \* \* \* \* \* \* \* \* \*

# VII

# CONFRATERNITIES OF OUR BLESSED LADY

These confraternities and sodalities have long been approved by holy Church to foster devotion, encourage prayer, urge their members to more frequent use of the Sacraments and promote the various spiritual and corporal works of mercy.

St. Francis de Sales and St. Charles Borromeo used confraternities extensively and with great efficacy in building up their dioceses in the face of spreading heresies.

\* \* \* \* \* \* \* \* \* \*

# VIII

# ALMS GIVEN IN MARY'S HONOR

Clients of the Blessed Virgin are accustomed to give alms to the poor in honor of the Blessed Mother, especially on Saturdays. St.

Gregory the Great encourages this practice in his *Dialogues*, and it was a favorite practice of St. Gerard.

\*   \*   \*   \*   \*   \*   \*   \*   \*   \*

## IX

## FREQUENT RECOURSE TO MARY

Of all devotions, there is none so pleasing to our Mother as that of having frequent recourse to her intercession, seeking her help in all our wants and needs. This can be the Hail Mary, the Memorare, some antiphon in her honor, or even the holy Names of Jesus and Mary.

\*   \*   \*   \*   \*   \*   \*   \*   \*   \*

## X

## OTHER PRACTICES IN HONOR OF MARY

1. To say or hear Mass, or have Mass celebrated, in honor of the Blessed Virgin. The holy sacrifice of the Mass can be offered to God alone, but the Council of Trent reminds us that this does not prevent us from offering it, at the same time, in honor of his special friends, Mary and the saints.
2. To reverence and honor the saints who are more nearly associated with Mary, as St. Joseph, SS Joachim and Anne, St. Elizabeth, St. John the Evangelist and St. John the Baptizer, St. Bernard, St. John Damascene, (and St. Alphonsus Liguori).
3. Every day read from some book that treats of the Blessed Mother, and then share this in preaching, teaching or just conversation. As the Blessed Virgin once said to St. Bridget: "Take care that your children are also my children."

# Conclusion

And with this, dear reader and client of Mother Mary, I bid you farewell. Continue with joy to honor and love this good Lady. Endeavor, also, to have her loved by as many as you can. And doubt not, that if you persevere until death in true devotion to Mary, your salvation is certain.

Accept, then, the desire which I had in this work, to lead you to salvation and to sanctify, by inflaming you with love and ardent devotion to this most amiable Queen.

And I turn to you in conclusion, O Mother of my Lord, and my Mother Mary. Graciously accept my poor labors and the desire which I have had to see you praised and loved by all.

You know how ardently I have desired to complete this little work of your Glories before the end of my life, which is already drawing to a close. But now I die happy, leaving this book on earth which will continue to praise and preach you as I have endeavored to do during the years which have passed since my conversion, which through you I obtained from God.

O Immaculate Mary, I recommend all those who love you to you, and especially those who read this little book. O Lady, grant them perseverance, make them all saints and lead them, thus united, to praise you in heaven.

I trust that in the agonies of death, when the devil will put my sins before me, that in the first place the Passion of Jesus, and then your intercession, will strengthen me and enable me to leave this miserable life in the grace of God, that so I may go and love Him, and thank you, my Mother for all eternity.    Amen.

# Index

John Paul II, Pope, 63
John the Baptizer, St., 125, 127, 141, 194
Joseph, St., 141, 154, 156, 175, 176, 180, 194
Justin Martyr, St., 76
Juvenal Ancino, Blessed, 99

Lawrence Justinian, St., 23, 28, 43, 56, 137, 151
Leo the Great, St., 93
Litany of Loretto, 191
Louis Bertrand, St., xx
Lucifer, 71
Luke, St., 8, 10, 17, 22, 23, 38, 46, 61, 65, 96, 111, 122, 123, 124, 126, 131, 132, 138, 152, 157, 163, 171, 172, 179, 180, 183

Maccabees, 55
Mary Magdalen, St., 125
Mary Magdalen de Pazzi, St., 91
Matilda, St., 32, 168
Matthew, St., 18, 59, 121, 154, 160, 168, 169, 175, 178
Mechtilde, St., 126
Mediator, 58
Mediatrix, 115
Methodius, St., 40, 67, 100, 111, 172, 173
Michael, Archangel, St., 31
Moses, 50, 131, 170
Mount Carmel, 87, 193

Noah, 24, 43, 75
Numbers, 50

Origen, 156
Our Lady of Grace, 127

Paul, St., 56, 95, 115, 131, 142, 175, 178, 182
Paul V, Pope, 86
Paulinus, St., 12

perseverance, 25, 30
Peter, St., 56
Peter Celestine, St., 187
Peter Chrysologus, St., 16
Peter Damian, St., 15, 31, 66, 78, 86, 99, 128, 170
Philip Neri, St., 15, 28, 177, 178
Pius V, Pope, 86
Pius IX, Pope, 113
Pius XII, Pope, 135
prayer, 17
presumption, 82
priests, xix, 35
Proverbs, 10, 14, 21, 26, 28, 29, 45, 56, 89, 129
Psalms, 27, 31, 40, 118, 133, 149, 160, 174
Purgatory, 27, 31, 40, 118, 133, 149, 160, 174

rainbow, 74, 75
Raymond Jordan, Blessed, 14, 61, 69, 100
Rebecca, 95
Redeemer, Holy, xvii, 11, 38, 48, 111, 120, 122, 148, 159
Redemptoris Mater, 63
Revelation, 13, 21, 30, 55, 56, 74, 96, 136, 137, 170
Robert Bellarmine, St., 10, 25, 36, 176
rosary, 32, 87, 191
Ruth, 43, 78

saints, 55, 56
Salve Regina, xv, xx, 15
Samuel, 50, 71
scapular, 87, 192
Seraphina of Capri, Ven., 90
Simeon, St., 132, 152, 162
Simon Stock, St., 193
sin, 7, 15, 16, 17, 18
Solomon, 74
Sophronius, St., 59, 112, 167, 176